DEAR ABBA

CLAIRE CLONINGER

DEAR ABBA

*Finding the Father's Heart
Through Prayer*

WORD PUBLISHING
Dallas·London·Vancouver·Melbourne

DEAR ABBA

Unless otherwise indicated, Scripture quotations are from the Holy Bible, New Century Version (NCV), copyright © 1987, 1988, 1991 by Word Publishing, Dallas, Texas 75234. Used by permission. Other Scripture references are from the following sources:

The Holy Bible, New International Version (NIV), copyright © 1973, 1978, 1984 by International Bible Society. Used by permission of Zondervan Publishing House. All rights reserved.

The Message (MSG), copyright © 1993. Used by permission of NavPress Publishing Group.

The King James Version of the Bible (KJV).

The New King James Version (NKJV), copyright © 1979, 1980, 1982, 1992, Thomas Nelson, Inc., Publisher.

J. B. Phillips: The New Testament in Modern English, revised edition (PHILLIPS). Copyright © J. B. Phillips 1958, 1960, 1972. Used by permission of Macmillan Publishing Co., Inc.

The Revised Standard Version of the Bible (RSV), copyrighted 1946, 1952, © 1971, 1973 by the Division of Christian Education of the National Council of the Churches of Christ in the U.S.A. Used by permission.

Published in association with the literary agency of Alive Communications, 1465 Kelly Johnson Blvd., Suite 320, Colorado Springs, Colorado 80920.

Library of Congress Cataloging-in-Publication Data
Cloninger, Claire.
Dear Abba : finding the father's heart through prayer / Claire Cloninger.
  p.   cm.
Includes bibliographical references.
ISBN 0-8499-1393-4
  1. Prayer—Christianity. 2. God—Love. 3. Spiritual exercises. I. Title.
BV215.C64   1997
248.3'2—dc21

                                                              97-9392
                                                                CIP

Printed in the United States of America
7 8 9 0 1 2 3 4 9 BVG 9 8 7 6 5 4 3 2 1

This book is lovingly dedicated to
Conlee and Signa Bodishbaugh,
fearless leaders of the CHRIST CHURCH PRAYER TEAM,
who have led us to listen to the Father more deeply
and experience him more fully.

And to the team members with whom I serve:
Susan and F. G. Baldwin,
Kirk and Deby Dearman,
Jacque Drane,
Nancy and Bob Gordon,
Brannon LaForce,
Kathy Maitre,
Pris and Bert Milling,
Leland Moore,
Marie Nickerson,
Tommy and Judy Oschwald,
Becky Patrick,
Jean Sherman,
Richard Weavill,
and
Lisa and Tom Yearwood.

How blessed I am to be part of
a faith community that prays!

CONTENTS

ACKNOWLEDGMENTS

So many people have given me practical, creative, and spiritual support in the writing of this book that I cannot possibly thank them all, but as I name these few, I pray that in some way they will stand in for all those I appreciate so much. I am thankful for my family members who support me in everything I undertake. For my husband, Spike, my sons and their wives, Curt and Julie, and Andy and Jenni. For my parents and all my siblings but especially my brother, Charlie, who has had special input in this project. I love you all.

For Tim Smith, my pastor; Pam Hanes, my friend and mentor; and John and Laura Barr, who continue to feed my spiritual fire. For the faithful prayers of many, especially Rebecca Morris, Ann Doige-Harrison, and the "Cuernavaca Six." For the organizational skills of Ginny Allen, my assistant.

For Laura Kendall at Word Publishing, who has "hung in there" with me on this idea; for Joey and Sharon Paul, who have believed in me; and for the expertise of Sue Ann Jones, my editor. For Greg Johnson, my agent at Alive Communications, whose suggestions have helped shape this book into its present form. And for Brennan

Manning, whose writing and teaching have helped blaze a trail for me to the heart of my Abba. Brennan, I will never forget the first day I heard you speak on Abba's love. It was Valentine's Day, 1977, at Little Sisters of the Poor in Mobile. You told me that the Abba of Jesus wanted me for his valentine, and I believed you. What a difference that has made!

A HUNGER FOR INTIMACY

In her 1979 acceptance speech for the Nobel prize, Mother Teresa of Calcutta told of visiting a handsomely furnished nursing home where elderly people had been placed by their adult children. Her initial impression was of the rich, attractive decor. And then she noticed the lifeless expression in the eyes of the home's residents. Accustomed to the smiles of "her people" in Calcutta, even the dying ones, the old nun was puzzled.

> I saw in that home they had everything, beautiful things, but everybody was looking toward the door. And I did not see a single one with a smile on their face. And I turned to the sister [in charge] and I asked: . . . "How is it that these people who have everything here, why are they all looking toward the door? Why are they not smiling?"

The sister in charge replied that these old people in their splendid setting were looking toward the door because they were "waiting," "expecting," hoping for a visit from a son or a daughter.

"They are hurt because they are forgotten," she added sadly.

Mother Teresa was reminded that day of something she had often observed in her work: that "the poorest of the poor" are not the only ones who know poverty. There is poverty in the midst of great wealth. There is loneliness in the middle of crowded rooms. And all of us are hungry. Even the well fed have a hunger of the heart.

It doesn't take a spiritual visionary like Mother Teresa to see the "heart hunger" in people around us. It's everywhere. People are hungry for a sense of significance, a sense of security, a sense of purpose. They need to know they are valued and loved for who they are. They are hungry for joy and peace and laughter. But behind all of these, I see the primary ache at the heart of the whole human family as a hunger for intimate relationship. All of us are looking toward the door for that One with whom we can intimately share our true selves.

A VARIETY OF SUBSTITUTES

Our culture holds out a variety of substitutes for intimacy:

- TV and videos parade the intimacy of fictional characters through our living rooms;

- radios pipe intimate love words of popular songs into our ears;

- magazines and newspapers convey the most intimate "true-life" details of the famous few;

- talk-show hosts trot out gruesome skeletons from a variety of dysfunctional-family closets for the daily shock effect their audiences have learned to love; and

- the Internet invites us to participate in the latest variety of substitutes for true intimacy, from screen-to-screen conversations to X-rated porn pages.

These counterfeits are plentiful and easily available, but they will never satisfy. Even our best and most rewarding human relationships cannot completely fill the hollow place in the human heart, for I am convinced that the true intimacy of a personal relationship with God is what each of us really hungers for. It's what we were made for, whether we know it or not. To share God's intimate love firsthand, to accept and internalize it, is to be released from our inner fortresses and our outer facades—released into the authentic life we were designed to embrace and contain.

From the pages of the Bible, from the beauty of creation, from the hidden rooms of our souls, the Father is calling us, his children, into intimate relationship. It is not a relationship bound up in rigid rule keeping. It is not some private religious club that bars potential members until they measure up. Quite the contrary! It is a relationship of grace, which calls us

- to stop running and allow ourselves to be "caught,"
- to stop pretending and allow ourselves to be known,
- to stop rushing and allow ourselves to be slowed down,
- to stop hiding and allow ourselves to be loved.

It is a relationship that calls us home to him from whatever far country our hearts have inhabited, from whatever love substitutes we've been relying on. Home—where our names are known and our gifts are celebrated.

How to Enter In

In many ways entering into an intimate friendship with the Father is like developing an intimate human relationship. Just as a love relationship with a spouse, a child, a parent, a dear friend is based on taking time to communicate honestly and listen actively, so is our relationship with God, to some extent, based on these things.

All true friendships change us, but our friendship with the Father, more than any other, has the potential to change us deeply. As we spend time in his loving, healing presence we will find ourselves growing in the ability to trust, to feel peace, to internalize grace, to experience joy, and to love others and ourselves.

The insights in this book can serve as road markers on your way to an intimate friendship with the Father. But ultimately that way must be traveled in prayer—your prayer. For drawing near to God requires more than merely reading. It requires praying.

There are many excuses for avoiding intimacy with God: the urgency of work, the pressures of other relationships, the busyness of daily life, and, ironically, even the demands of ministry. But one of the greatest roadblocks to an intimate life of prayer is simply failing to begin, for ultimately, prayer is learned by praying. That is why this book moves beyond what you think about praying to a doorway where you can enter in. It contains daily Scripture-inspired opportunities for you to hear from God, as well as opportunities to respond in prayer to what you have heard.

The Best Way to Use This Book

This is a simple book that is simple to use. Each of its ten chapters guides you into another avenue of prayer, another aspect of relating to your heavenly Father. As you read, ask the Holy Spirit to show you who God is. Ask him to open the deep messages of God's Word. Then remain open to his spiritual "nudges." What could be more exciting than to form a friendship with our amazing Creator! How awesome to realize that he is trying to reveal to you the secrets of his heart and his purposes for your life!

As you use this book, the basis of your developing friendship with the Father will be a "correspondence" with him. I have found that writing out my letters to God in journal form over the past twenty years has been for me one of the most valuable ways of experiencing a personal relationship with God.

Dear Abba is designed as a ten-week devotional adventure. After each of the ten chapters there are five Scripture-inspired "love letters" from God to you. You will be reading these letters, approximately one per day, and reflecting on God's personal message to you. Then you will be guided in writing your own letter to him in a separate journal or in the space provided.

I feel led to add here that if you need or desire to spend more than ten weeks on the material in this book, by all means do! Don't rush the Spirit of God. He is not trying to hurry you through a crash course in knowing the Father! He's got all eternity, after all, and so do you!

NO WRONG WORDS

In the letters you will write, there are no wrong words. Whatever you want to say to God is what God wants to hear.

One of the most important prerequisites to true intimacy is complete honesty. As C. S. Lewis said, we should "lay before Him what is in us, not what ought to be in us."[1]

The Father is pleased that you are willing to come to him as his child and spend time with him, so come as naturally and unselfconsciously as you can. Don't overspiritualize your thoughts or feelings. If you are hurting, say so. If you are confused, seek his guidance. If your joy is bubbling over, let it bubble over in praise.

If you bring to these simple devotionals as much honesty and openness as you can, I can almost guarantee that you will find your prayer life richer and your relationship with the Father deeper by the time you close this book and set it down.

A Note to the Reader

I do not know you, so I cannot know how this book came to be in your hands. But I believe with all my heart that God meant for you to read these words today, for they contain an invitation with your name on it. It is an invitation to communicate one-on-one with the Creator of the whole universe, who calls you his child. It is your chance to talk to him with utter honesty, to listen to him with simple faith, and to discover that he is the God who still relates intimately to his children if they will open their hearts and invite him in. It is an invitation to put down the heaviness you carry and know the deep rest of being a beloved child in your Father's house.

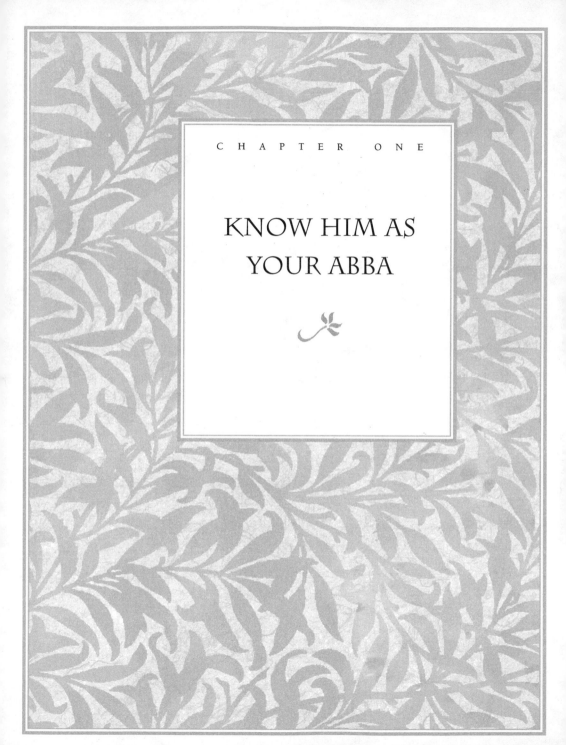

CHAPTER ONE

KNOW HIM AS
YOUR ABBA

KNOW HIM AS YOUR ABBA

My friend Pris returned to college recently and was delighted to discover that she could take four religion courses as electives. When I called her shortly after her first semester had begun, I could hardly wait to hear about the Old Testament elective she had been so excited about.

"How's the class?" I asked, expecting an enthusiastic response.

"Well," she hesitated, "it's okay, I guess, but I sometimes feel I could learn more about relating to God in a preschool Sunday school class. College courses about God get so convoluted and removed from the reality of who he really is."

Which got me to thinking. Who is he, really? Who is he to theologians? To preschoolers? Who is he in your life? In mine? Pursue those questions with me now as we picture two very different scenes.

In scene one, you are sitting in a gleaming, handsomely appointed reception area, waiting to be interviewed for a job—a job for which you feel vastly underqualified. You have shamelessly tweaked your resume in an effort to make yourself sound better than you feel you are. While waiting, you look down and discover a large, dull stain on your suit jacket. Oh well, too late to do anything about that. You look around, surveying the competition. Three attractive, professional-looking business types are seated around you, each with an enviable air of poise and confidence. Suddenly you find yourself wishing you could bolt. Whatever made you think you could pull this off?

But at that very moment, the receptionist calls your name and ushers you into an oak-paneled office where you are seated before a stern-looking gentleman in a well-cut suit who asks, "So, tell me why you feel you'd be right for this position."

That's scene number one.

Now, scene number two. It is your birthday. You have just returned from a two-mile run, and you realize you're actually in better shape than you were five years ago! You're humming in the shower, looking forward to meeting a close friend for lunch at a favorite restaurant. Clean hair, clean jeans, great outlook, beautiful day. The maitre d' seats you in a sunny, inside dining room. Suddenly out pop not one but five of your favorite friends, laughing and shrieking, "Surprise!" After lunch and cake, crazy gifts, and cards, five glasses of watery iced tea are lifted to toast you. One by one, each friend tells you why he or she is so grateful to God for your friendship.

AN ALL-IMPORTANT QUESTION

No need to ask you which scene is more appealing! You'd have to be a masochist to choose scene number one. But I want to pose a much more telling question. Of the two scenes, which one reminds you more of your relationship with God? Think about it.

Is your time with him like a tense interview for a job you might not get? Is he someone with whom you're always nervously trying to act better than you are because you fear your real self might not be good enough? Or do you see your relationship with God as time spent with your very best friend? When you're with him do you feel welcomed and valued and totally loved?

"To think rightly about God is, in an important sense, to have everything right," says Richard Foster. "To think wrongly about God is, in an important sense, to have everything wrong."[1] "Nothing twists and deforms the soul more than a low or unworthy conception of God," wrote A. W. Tozer.[2]

The crux of Christianity, the open door to life that lasts forever, is knowing who God really is. ("Now this is eternal life: that they may know you, the only true God, and Jesus Christ, whom you have sent"—John 17:3 NIV.)

For this reason, knowing God must be the initial assignment in a life of prayer. We can't expect to have an intimate relationship with someone we don't know. We will never come in childlike faith to someone we don't trust. And so I invite you now to begin at the beginning with me and consider, Who is this God to whom we pray?

I would not presume to tell you in a few paragraphs or pages exactly who God is. Whole libraries are devoted to warehousing the books on that subject. And yet as his child I can tell you from the heart of my experience that he is a good Father who cares for his children, and he is a faithful Friend who has never let me down in the more than twenty years I have walked with him. I can also take you to his Word, where we as little children can begin to follow the clues that lead us to encounter him face to face.

AN INTIMATE NAME

Jesus gave us a major clue to God's identity when his disciples asked, "Master, teach us to pray."

"When you pray," he said, in effect, "do it this way: 'Our Father . . .'" (see Matt. 6). This must have shocked and scandalized many in the crowd who were accustomed to picturing God as a sometimes harsh and always distant deity.

But Jesus used an even more intimate name to speak to his Father (see Mark 14:36). He used the name "Abba," the name of affection a little Hebrew child would use for a beloved parent, just as a child in our culture might say "Daddy" or "Papa." By calling God "Abba," Jesus was telling us something important about God's nature and character. He was identifying God as a loving and approachable parent, a "dad." And this childlike name of affection was not reserved for Jesus alone. We who follow him are given the Spirit, which calls us into the same kind of relationship Jesus had— one in which we may refer to God as "Abba" or "Daddy" (see Gal. 4:6 and Rom. 8:15 (NIV)).

Learning to think of God as a good and dependable "Dad" comes easier for some than others. My friend Eve, who grew up in a broken home, had a difficult time seeing God this way. Her parents divorced when she was very young, and she rarely saw her father. Eve's mother, who never really recovered from the loss, became chronically depressed, introverted, and childlike. Eve learned at an early age to function as the adult in the family. If a dress was needed for a school function or pictures for a yearbook, she made those arrangements herself.

When Eve became a Christian, a relationship with Jesus as Friend and Savior felt natural to her. But relaxing into a father-child relationship with a heavenly Father who would meet her needs felt extremely difficult. She had never known a parent like that. She felt no freedom to approach God, no confidence to ask for what she needed. Eve had been "on her own" for so long that she needed to have her whole idea of "father" transformed before she could trust God.

Like Eve, most of us relate to God as we did to our earthly parents—especially our fathers. Our ability to trust and be intimate with God is often determined by the amount of trust and intimacy we experienced with our earthly "dad." If we had good, stable, loving earthly fathers who were available and supportive, we find intimacy with the Father easy. If our earthly fathers were frequently absent, if they were negligent, abusive, or emotionally distant, intimacy with God is much, much harder.

GOD'S LONGING FOR INTIMACY

God knows what kind of childhood each of us had. He understands the reasons we may feel far from him. He longs to heal our misconceptions of what a father should be so that we can know him as he is and enter into a Father-child relationship with him.

Eugene Petersen's paraphrase of Romans 8:15 in *The Message* describes the intimacy of such a relationship.

> This resurrection life you received from God is not a timid, grave-tending life. It's adventurously expectant, greeting God with a childlike, "What's next, Papa?" God's spirit touches our spirits and confirms who we really are. We know who he is, and we know who we are: Father and children.

AN INVITATION TO COME TO HIM

Several years ago I participated in a hilarious but touching session with actress Jeanette Clift George that beautifully illustrates the loving invitation God extends to all of us. In this session Jeanette invited members of the audience to help her act out her understanding of how Jesus' death on Calvary had removed any obstacles in the relationship between God and his children.

She began by setting up a little area on the stage that she called "the Holy of Holies."

"This is where the Lord dwells," she explained, "and the only human being ever allowed here in this little room where the Lord dwells is the great high priest." (She then called someone out of the audience to play the role of the high priest.)

Next Jeanette marked off a place just beyond the great veil of the Holy of Holies where other less-important priests waited for the high priest to reveal to them what the Lord had said. She selected audience members to stand in that area as the less-important priests.

Beyond this, Jeanette stationed a group of audience members to represent the men of the twelve tribes who would receive the word of the Lord from the priests. And beyond that, she enlisted some of us to represent Jewish women who waited in the outer courts of the temple for their fathers and husbands and sons to come out and convey God's message to them.

And finally, way, way outside the temple wall altogether was an area where Jeanette placed a few straggling audience members to represent any Gentiles who might possibly have waited to hear a fifth-hand proclamation of what the Hebrew God had to say. Gentile men would have stood closest to the temple wall, and then women.

"So this would have been *my* place," Jeanette told us, "way out here, away from God's heart, on the total back row of everything!"

And then she began to tell about the coming of Jesus Christ to earth for all the different strata of humanity who were waiting outside the Father's heart of hearts. She told how for the love of us he was nailed to a cross and died and laid in a tomb and raised to new life on the third day. And she told how in that act, that sacrifice, Jesus had cut a clear path through the crowds of people. He had ripped from top to bottom the veil that had shrouded the Holy of Holies. And he had exposed the very heart of God to anyone who wanted to know him intimately and love him totally.

As Jeanette described the beautiful gift of Calvary to her audience, she began to move through the levels of people standing outside the Holy of Holies.

"'Scuse me," she said to the Gentile women and the Gentile men as she began to make her way from the back of the crowd to the heart of God.

"Pardon me," she said to the Jewish women and the Jewish men as she moved closer still.

"Excuse me, may I get through here?" she asked the crowd of priests still mingling outside the Holy of Holies.

And then she gingerly pushed back the ripped veil and stepped inside the holiest place in all the world, the intimate dwelling place of God Almighty.

As she crawled up on the altar, she turned to the high priest who was standing there, indignantly looking at her with an expression of total shock.

"We'd like to be alone now, if you don't mind," she said to the high priest. He hurried away, outraged.

Sitting all alone now in God's presence, Jeanette folded her hands in her lap and looked up to heaven with the sweetest, most childlike expression on her face and said, "Hi, God. It's me, Jeanette."

Throughout all my years as a Christian, Jeanette's delightful drama remains one of the most vivid images I have ever seen of the intimate relationship Jesus made available to us by his sacrifice. In that drama I saw clearly that God is here, unveiled and waiting to welcome any one of us who is willing to come to him.

This invitation for relationship extends across the board. People of all ages, races, IQs, and economic groups are welcomed into his presence and warmed by his constant friendship, just as they have been over centuries and generations, because his love is available to all of us, from theology professors to preschoolers who can't even spell their names!

FOUNDATIONAL WORD PICTURES

Seeing clearly into the Father heart of God and understanding his ever-available love for us is one of the most life-changing visions our hearts will ever hold. Gaining this intimate picture of God as Abba is a foundational step on the Christian journey.

The word *foundational* brings up an image in my mind. My husband and I live in a log cabin, which we built with our own hands. But before we ever lifted a log, we had a professional construction crew build the foundation, because we realized that had the foundation been even a little bit off, our whole cabin would have been lopsided (or, as my mother-in-law, Marjie, used to say, "womper-jawed"). It's the same with our faith. If we do not have a foundational understanding of God as a loving Father, it doesn't matter what theological logs of learning we may add; our faith will always be "womper-jawed."

A Higher Love

Part of this foundational understanding is realizing that, unlike our earthly parents who were limited in their ability to love, God is unlimited. Unlike our earthly parents who may have wounded and/or disappointed us, God's love will never disappoint.

Isaiah 49:15 asks this question: "Can a mother forget the baby at her breast and have no compassion on the child she has borne?" And then it answers its own question. "Though she may forget, I will not forget you! See, I have engraved you on the palms of my hands" (NIV).

I breast-fed both of my sons, and I can testify to the fact that a mother cannot easily forget the child she is breast-feeding. The baby's feeding schedule becomes intimately linked with the mother's "inner clock," and his slightest cry, even from the next room, will cause the mother's milk to come in. God planned it this way, as a built-in physiological alarm clock.

But can a mother lack kindness toward her children? We only have to watch the nightly news to be reminded that it happens every day.

And yet, God is saying to us in this passage: "Even though your mother should lack love and have no compassion . . . even though your father should hurt or harm you . . . even though they should forget you and turn their backs, I, your God, your Abba, your heavenly parent, will not forget you. See, I have engraved you on the palms of my hands!"

I believe that in some mysterious way our names were carved into the palms of God's hands by the nails of the cross. The sacrificial death of his Son on Calvary has written us into his life in such a way that he can never, never forget us. He is our Father, and we are his children. This is a foundational understanding regarding the character of God, an understanding that can revolutionize our faith in him and change the lives we live as his children.

THE DETERMINING QUESTION

At a Christian music conference in Colorado some years ago, I heard

Brennan Manning state his belief that when we leave this life and stand in God's presence, we will only be asked one question. *What would that question be? I wondered. Aren't we supposed to give an answer for everything at the judgment seat of Christ?*

"I believe," Brennan continued, "the only question God will have to ask is, 'Did you believe that I loved you . . . that I waited for you and longed to hear the sound of your voice?'"

Think about it. The answer that we are able to give to that question at the end of our lives will effectively answer who we have become. For if we have truly known and internalized the gentle, yearning love of our Papa-God, how could we have lived anything but loving lives in response?

Jesus spent his whole ministry trying to get his followers to know the God he called "Abba." His little roadside "theology courses" painted God not as some far-off, inaccessible deity, but as a Shepherd who searched tirelessly for a lost sheep, as a loving Dad who waited with forgiveness on his lips to welcome home a wayward child. These stories are simple but powerful lessons that call us into the waiting arms of a great mercy.

In fact, the whole redemptive mission of Jesus might be viewed as making a way for us to come into his Abba's presence with childlike confidence. He was, in a sense, placing the small hand of humanity in the great, kind hand of its Creator and saying, "Child, come, and know your Father."

This is the very same mission I feel in my heart as I write this book. So many people I talk to and pray with (even many who identify themselves as "saved," "committed," or "born again") feel emotionally distanced from the tender Parent who yearns for an intimate relationship with them. Many of them attend church, contribute time and money toward kingdom purposes, even pray faithfully, but they have trouble hearing God's still, small voice that speaks with the accent of love.

"He Wasn't My Dad"

Our friend Mike Scanland spent the early part of his Christian journey feeling emotionally distanced from God. Mike grew up with no father in his life after the age of four, and as a child, he often daydreamed about his dad's return.

On the high school football field during practice or a game, as he looked enviously at the fathers of other players sitting in the stands cheering for their sons, Mike would wonder where his father was.

Then one day during practice, a stranger came ambling toward the field, looking intently at the players. The thought suddenly entered Mike's mind that this must surely be his dad. *He's finally found out where I am, and he's come for me!* Mike thought. But instead of stopping, the stranger just walked on by.

"My heart sank inside me," Mike said, remembering that painful moment. "Whoever this guy was, he wasn't my dad. My dad was out there somewhere, all right, but he was unavailable to me. I think that was the moment I must have made the connection between God and my dad. They represented everything I needed. They were vital to me, but they were both a long way out of my reach."

A Parable of Abba Love

If there's something inside you that believes, as Mike did, that God is distant or uncaring, your heart needs healing. If the home where you learned about love was not loving, you need to know the Papa-God who loves you totally, who wants the best for you, who forgives you the moment you confess and has an endless supply of new beginnings when you are at a dead end.

But for me to attempt to describe God's all-powerful, unconditional love is to experience the frustrations of the limits of language. All the brightest adjectives and highest superlatives seem pale and anemic when I try to say who he is to me. So when descriptions fail, I fall back on an old reliable communicating technique that Jesus himself often used—the parable.

This particular parable actually happened at the 1992 Olympics in Barcelona, Spain. That year Great Britain had a runner named Derek Redmond who had dreamed all his life of winning the gold medal in the four-hundred-meter race. As the gun sounded for the semifinals, Derek knew that his dream was in view and he was running the race of his life.

Then, tragically, as he entered the backstretch, Redmond felt a rip of pain shoot up the back of his right leg. A torn right hamstring sent him sprawling facedown on the hard surface of the track.

By an act of sheer determination, Derek struggled to his feet in excruciating pain and began crazily hopping on one leg toward the finish line. Later he would tell reporters it was as though an animal instinct took over. He knew he had to finish the race!

Suddenly a large man in a T-shirt came bounding out of the stands. Flinging aside security guards, he made his way onto the field and threw his arms around Derek. It was Jim Redmond, Derek's father.

"Son, you don't have to do this," he said.

"Yes, Dad, I do," Derek assured him.

"All right then, let's finish this thing together," said the older man. And that's exactly what they did. Staying in Derek's lane the whole way, the son's head frequently buried in the father's shoulder, they made it to the end of the race as the crowd rose to its feet, weeping and cheering![3]

Derek Redmond did not win the gold medal in the Olympics. But I believe he won something far more valuable. He walked away from the race with the memory of a father who was not only in the stands cheering but who loved him too much to watch him suffer from a distance—a father who came down out of the stands and entered the race with him, staying beside him every step of the way.

YOUR EARTHLY FATHER, YOUR HEAVENLY ABBA

I don't know what kind of earthly father you had. You may have had a loving and supportive dad like Derek Redmond's. You may have had a father who disappeared from your life when you were very young like Mike's father did. Maybe it was death or divorce or illness or addiction that kept him from being the kind of parent you needed. Perhaps he was well-meaning but frequently absent due to long working hours. Perhaps he was inconsistent or negligent or even blatantly abusive.

But whatever our earthly fathers may have been like, it's so important for each of us to know that from the beginning we have had a heavenly Abba who was in the stands watching us with eyes of affection, pulling for us at every turn in our lives. He is our Papa-God who cared for us too deeply to stay in heaven, looking down on us, watching us fall and fail. Instead, he came down out of the stands and into our race in the person of his precious Son, Jesus Christ. And he is committed to staying in this race with us until we have safely crossed the finish line.

CORRESPONDING WITH YOUR ABBA GOD

In the five spiritual exercises that follow, and in those after each chapter, you will be "corresponding" with Abba God by using your prayer journal. The focus of each day's exercise is knowing God as your Abba.

In the verses of Scripture and in each letter from God, listen for his voice of love and look for clues to his character. As you respond to his letters, be as honest and open as you possibly can. Use your own words. Be yourself. God wants to have an intimate personal relationship with the real you.

KNOW HIM AS YOUR ABBA: 1

SEE ME AS I AM

*Read and reflect on these verses of Scripture
and the letter from your Abba that follows.*

I will comfort you as a mother comforts her child. Isa. 66:13A

Praise be to the God and Father of our Lord Jesus Christ. God is the Father who is full of mercy and all comfort. 2 Cor. 1:3

Can a woman forget the baby she nurses? Can she feel no kindness for the child to which she gave birth? Even if she could forget her children, I will not forget you. See, I have written your name on my hand. Isa. 49:15

He surrounded them and brought them up, guarding them as those he loved very much. He was like an eagle building its nest that flutters over its young. Deut. 32:10B

Dear Child,

Open the eyes of your heart and see me as I am. I am the Father who longs to draw you near, to comfort you with tenderness when you are lonely or afraid, to shield you with care when you cry out to me, to shelter you and protect you as an eagle protects its young. Though this world is clouded with mixed messages and diluted commitments, my message is clear. My commitment is certain. I love you. You are mine. Though human love is not always consistent, my love is as sure as the sunrise. I am here for you and will be here. Though others may forget you, I never will. Your name has been carved into the palms of my open hands and your face is ever before me. You are my child. Will you choose to believe that?

I am your,
Abba

WRITE A LETTER TO YOUR ABBA: 1

PRAYERS OF A CHILD

After reading and reflecting on God's words to you, write your own letter to him in your journal or in the space below, using the following guide:

1. In your journal or in the space below, write a letter to Abba God, confessing any way your heart may be closed to receiving the love he is expressing to you. Ask him to help you open your heart to believe and receive the truth of who he is.

Dear Abba,

_____

_____

_____

_____

_____

_____

2. Now put your pen down. Ask Abba God to speak to you. Sit quietly for ten minutes (or more) and listen for him in your heart. What is he saying to you about who he is? What personal words of love, guidance, or challenge do you hear? Write these out in your journal. (Remember, God's word in your heart will never conflict with his revealed Word in the Bible.)

CLOSING PRAYER: *Abba God, thank you for desiring a relationship with me. I admit that it's difficult for me to understand a love like yours, and sometimes it is hard to receive. But I am so grateful for what you are revealing to me about who you are. Help me to draw closer to you. Amen.*

KNOW HIM AS YOUR ABBA: 2

I AM YOUR PEACE

A very strong wind came up on the lake. The waves came over the sides and into the boat so that it was already full of water. Jesus was at the back of the boat, sleeping with his head on a cushion. His followers woke him and said, "Teacher, don't you care that we are drowning!" Jesus stood up and commanded the wind and said to the waves, "Quiet! Be still!" Then the wind stopped, and it became completely calm. MARK 4:37-39

> Those who go to God Most High for safety
>   will be protected by the Almighty. . . .
> He will cover you with his feathers,
>   and under his wings you can hide.
>   His truth will be your shield and protection. Ps. 91:1, 4

Christ himself is our peace. EPH. 2:14

My Own Dear Child,

Even in the midst of great turmoil, I am your peace. When your emotions are in a tangle and you can't put your finger on that nagging "something" that won't let you go, bring your troubled heart to me. I will comb through the conflicts, quiet the inner confusion, and put my holy hand on the very thing you need to deal with. When the winds of this world bear down upon the sanctuary of your heart, threatening to tear it apart, tuck your life up under my wing and rest in me. My peace is more powerful than the conflicts of this life. I will be the stillness at the center of your storm.

> *This I promise you!*
> *Abba*

WRITE A LETTER TO YOUR ABBA: 2

PRAYERS OF A CHILD

1. In your letter, tell God about any areas of conflict or confusion in your life. Invite his healing presence into these areas and see his peace permeating your whole being.

   Dear Abba,

   _____

   _____

   _____

   _____

   _____

   _____

   _____

   _____

   _____

2. Now put down your pen. Ask Abba God to speak to you. Sit quietly for ten minutes (or more) and listen for him in your heart. What is he saying to you about his peace? What personal words of love, guidance, or challenge do you hear? Write these out in your journal. (Remember, God's word in your heart will never conflict with his revealed Word in the Bible.)

   CLOSING PRAYER: *Dear Abba, thank you that you are still in the business of calming storms. I need you to come in and calm mine. Forgive me when I try to handle everything myself. Help me to stay consciously aware of your nearness. And when I feel the confusion of life closing in, help me to stop and call on you. Amen.*

KNOW HIM AS YOUR ABBA: 3

WILL YOU OPEN THE DOOR?

Behold, I stand at the door and knock; if any one hears my voice and opens the door, I will come in to him and eat with him, and he with me.
REV. 3:20 (RSV)

Dear Child,

I look into your life to a place of loneliness. Do you really think that no one knows you—that no one cares? You are not alone, my child. I am here, much closer to you than you know, and I care for you deeply. I stand just outside your heart, knocking and waiting for you to invite me in. I long to spend time with you—to guide and comfort you, to help you over every obstacle. I want you to know me as your Abba. I wait for you to open the door of your heart to my friendship so you can share your life with me. As you do, you will discover an amazing secret. Just being in my presence each day will radically change things for you. It will add a dimension of purpose and joy to your life that nothing else can duplicate.

Will you open the door to my love?
Abba

WRITE A LETTER TO YOUR ABBA: 3

PRAYERS OF A CHILD

1. See yourself opening the door of your heart to the Lord. In writing, ask him in. Will you show him all of the rooms—the rooms where you feel secure and the rooms where you have suffered rejection? The rooms you have "cleaned up" and the rooms that you keep behind closed doors? Write about God's visit to your heart. What was his reaction to your inner self? What did you learn about him? Write these things in your journal.

Dear Abba,

_____

_____

_____

_____

2. Now put down your pen. Ask Abba to speak to you. Sit quietly for ten minutes (or more) and listen to him in your heart. What is he saying to you about how your openness to him can change you? What personal words of love, guidance, or challenge do you hear? Write these out in your journal. (Remember, God's word in your heart will never conflict with his revealed Word in the Bible.)

CLOSING PRAYER: *Dear Abba, forgive me for the times I have kept you locked out of my heart. Thank you for pursuing me and for not giving up. I want you to be at home in every room of my heart. I don't want to hide anything from you. Teach me to trust you more and more. Amen.*

KNOW HIM AS YOUR ABBA: 4

MY LOVE IS CONSISTENT AND STRONG

He is like a rock; what he does is perfect,
and he is always fair.
He is a faithful God who does no wrong,
who is right and fair. DEUT. 32:4

If we are not faithful, he will still be faithful, because he cannot be false
to himself. 2 TIM. 2:13

Jesus Christ is the same yesterday, today, and forever. HEB. 13:8

Dear Child,

*So few things in your world are steady. The newspapers reveal the ups
and downs of a shifting, changing society. Politics, economics, technology,
social customs, clothing styles—so many things fluctuate that you may feel
at times there is nothing consistent you can count on. Human love can also
be a changing thing, at times leaving you wounded and betrayed. In the
midst of all these changes, I am the unchanging God, the same through
all generations, yesterday, today, and forever. My promises will never
waver or vary. My Word will stay constant to the last dot of the last i.
My commitment to you is total, and my love for you is unshakable. I am
asking you to believe this with all your being. Let the roots of your spirit
go down deep into the soil of my unchanging love.*

I am here for you,
Abba

WRITE A LETTER TO YOUR ABBA: 4

PRAYERS OF A CHILD

1. In your letter, tell Abba God about a relationship in which you feel you were loved inconsistently. Reflect on God's letter to you that you have just read. What is he promising you that is different from the inconsistent relationship you have described? List the qualities of faithfulness found in the Scripture verses and in his letter. Thank him for those qualities of love.

Dear Abba,

_____

_____

_____

_____

_____

_____

_____

2. Now put down your pen. Ask Abba God to speak to you. Sit quietly for ten minutes (or more) and listen for him in your heart. What is he saying to you about his changeless love? What personal words of love, guidance, or challenge do you hear? Write these out in your journal. (Remember, God's word in your heart will never conflict with his revealed Word in the Bible.)

CLOSING PRAYER: *Dear Abba, it is hard to imagine a love as faithful and unchanging as yours. Help me to overcome any doubts that hold me back from receiving you as you are. Give me an inner assurance that you are always with me. Amen.*

KNOW HIM AS YOUR ABBA: 5

I WILL USE IT FOR GOOD

We know that in everything God works for the good of those who love him. They are the people he called, because that was his plan. ROM. 8:28

So I went down to the potter's house, and saw him working at the potter's wheel. He was using his hands to make a pot from clay, but something went wrong with it. So he used that clay to make another pot the way he wanted it to be. Then the LORD spoke his word to me: "Family of Israel, can't I do the same thing with you?" says the LORD. "You are in my hands like the clay in the potter's hands." JER. 18:3–6

My Dear Child,

I want you to know that I see what you are going through, and I am at work in the midst of it. In that very situation that has caused you restless days and sleepless nights, I am at work. In that very conflict that has at times seemed hopeless, in that very relationship that has caused you pain, I am at work. You are my child, precious to me, called for my purposes, set aside for my plans. That is why I will bring good from the bad things in your life. When the destructive forces of this fallen world conspire against you, know that I am on your side. When troubling circumstances seem stacked against you, know that I am greater than any circumstance. Just as the potter can take the ruined pot and reshape it into a new vessel for a new use, I can take that painful circumstance in your life and reshape it for a new and glorious purpose.

I love you,
Abba

WRITE A LETTER TO YOUR ABBA: 5

PRAYERS OF A CHILD

1. In your journal or in the space below, write a letter to Abba God about a difficult circumstance you are dealing with in your life right now. Is there some "hopeless-looking" situation that needs to be redeemed by his love? Give God permission to take and reshape that situation, drawing good from the bad.

   Dear Abba,

   _____

   _____

   _____

   _____

   _____

   _____

2. Now put down your pen. Ask Abba God to speak to you. Sit quietly for ten minutes (or more) and listen for him in your heart. What is he saying to you about his ability to draw good from the bad things in your life? What personal words of love, guidance, or challenge do you hear? Write these out in your journal. (Remember, God's word in your heart will never conflict with his revealed Word in the Bible.)

   CLOSING PRAYER: *Dear Abba, it is easy to see difficult situations as impossible obstacles, especially when I look no deeper than the surface. Help me to remember that you are at work beneath the surface in even the most hopeless-looking things. Teach me to see the possibilities hiding inside the problems. Amen.*

CHAPTER TWO

LET HIM HAVE YOUR LIFE

LET HIM HAVE YOUR LIFE

Some years ago, when public speaking felt much more risky for me than it does now, I found myself at Word Music's annual sales conference, scheduled to speak but totally unprepared. My struggle to come up with an inspiring message had yielded only a trash basket filled with crumpled paper.

By the time I arrived at the conference, I was desperate. After a session of frenzied pacing, I ended up on the floor of my hotel room, facedown. While I was there (with my nose literally smushed into the patterned maroon pile of the carpet, crying, "Lord, I can't, I can't, I can't!") I heard a still, small, inner voice saying, "You're right. You can't. But I can. Are you willing to risk that?"

Willing to risk, to be out of control, to feel foolish if things didn't go the way I thought they should? I have to admit, the very prospect made my knees feel like Jell-O. It was like standing on a ledge. But it began gradually to dawn on me that this was a familiar ledge, one on which I had stood before.

"Okay, Lord, I'm willing," I whispered. And suddenly I was overwhelmed by a great wave of peace. He had something to say through me, and if I would just loan him my heart and my voice, he would do it.

I began to weep. It suddenly seemed so obvious. Wasn't this the way I was meant to live on a daily basis? Why did I always wait so long to let go?

AN AMAZING PEACE

I wish I could report to you that the talk I gave that day was the best I'd ever given. But I can't, because I honestly can't remember. I wrote down a few notes, looked up a few Scriptures, walked into a crowded amphitheater, and began to speak. It wasn't hard. It was very simple. And when it was over, it was over. I didn't go back and say to myself, *How did I do? How did they respond?* I just smiled and said, "Thanks, Lord," and walked out with an awesome sense of peace.

What a way to live! And to think that that quality of serenity and inner joy is available to each of us every day that we are willing to surrender. What, then, keeps us from taking advantage of it?

I think I can answer that question. Surrendering requires letting go, and letting go is very uncomfortable. It flies in the face of everything we've been taught by this culture—this culture whose twin national anthems seem to be "I Gotta Be Me" and "I Did It My Way." Most of us have been schooled in the art of being in control, living as captains of our own destinies, architects of our own life plans. Many of us find the old anxiety level rising sharply at the thought of being caught without a "to-do" list, without a mapped-out agenda. We feel much more comfortable with marching orders, job descriptions, and mission statements so that little is left to chance. We want our priorities neatly listed and our lives tidily contained.

A STRAITJACKET OF CONTROL

But our desire for control can easily become a straitjacket, as it was in the life of a lovely young woman I'll call Robin, who came to me for prayer. Robin was convinced that her problem was her husband's alcoholism.

"I've done everything I can possibly think of to get him to change," she told me. "I've begged, reasoned, prayed, nagged, manipulated, threatened, and given ultimatums. I just don't know what else to do."

"Have you tried giving up?" I asked her.

"What do you mean?" She looked puzzled.

"I mean have you considered letting go of your husband's problem and putting it in God's hands? Have you thought of giving up on trying to change him and allowing God to begin changing you?"

Robin became extremely agitated at my suggestion. As we prayed, I encouraged her to let God have her struggle, but sadly, she couldn't seem to let go.

"It's no good," she finally sighed. "It's impossible. I've been in control all my life, and asking me to let go is like asking me to jump off a cliff."

Free-Falling into the Unknown

In some way, to a greater or lesser degree, all of us are like Robin. We've been trying to be in control for so long that voluntarily relinquishing that control to an invisible God feels like jumping off the edge of all that is certain and free-falling into the unknown. It's scary, but we'll never find the faith adventure until we do. We'll never discover the surprising joy of living for the Lord until we are willing to surrender to his agenda and let him call the shots.

Surrender is always the primary action of the faith life. It was the action Abraham took when he left the familiarity of the land he knew and set out toward a land he had never seen. It was the action Esther took when she left the safety of the harem to confront her husband, the king, and plead for the safety of her people. It was the action the fishermen-disciples took when they left their nets and followed Jesus. And it is the action each of us must take if we hope to live the life of faith.

For not only is surrender the primary action, it is also the perpetual action of the faith adventure. It is something we do for the first time when we surrender our hearts and lives to Jesus Christ to receive salvation. And it is a choice we make over and over again at every small crossroads as we follow him.

THE CALL TO SURRENDER

The challenge to "let go and let God" comes to everyone who desires a relationship with him. It comes dressed in its own unique set of circumstances for each of us, but it calls to us with the same kind of message. It says: "Trust me, for only I can handle this person, this relationship, this situation, this job, this disease, this addiction, this financial problem.

"Will you take your hands off and trust me? Will you let me be God? Let go of whatever it is. I am waiting to take control."

Surrendering the Handlebars

If I do choose to surrender to God, what exactly am I called to let go of? The first and most essential struggle is over my right to have things my way, my right to steer my own life. When I surrender to God, I am putting those "rights" in his hands. In short, I am trading my will for his. This is a decision both terrifying and exhilarating in its riskiness, as this excerpt from a favorite poem of mine vividly portrays.

> When I met Christ
> it seemed as though life were rather like a bike ride,
> but it was a tandem bike,
> and I noticed that Christ
> was in the back helping me pedal.
>
> I don't know just when it was
> that He suggested we change places,
> but life has not been the same since.
>
> When I had control, I knew the way,
> It was rather boring, but predictable . . .
> It was the shortest distance between two points.
>
> But when He took the lead,
> He knew delightful long cuts,

up mountains, and through rocky places
at breakneck speeds,
it was all I could do to hang on!
Even though it looked like madness,
He said, "Pedal!"

I worried and was anxious and asked,
"Where are you taking me?"
He laughed and didn't answer,
and I started to learn to trust.

I forgot my boring life
and entered into the adventure.
And when I'd say, "I'm scared,"
He'd lean back and touch my hand.

He took me to people with gifts that I needed,
gifts of healing, acceptance, and joy.
He said, "Give the gifts away;
they're extra baggage, too much weight."
So I did, to the people we met,
and I found that in giving I received,
and still our burden was light.

I did not trust Him, at first,
in control of my life.
I thought He'd wreck it;
but He knows bike secrets,
knows how to make it bend to take sharp corners,

knows how to jump to clear high rocks,
knows how to fly to shorten scary passages.

And I am learning to shut up and pedal
in the strangest places,
and I'm beginning to enjoy the view
and the cool breeze on my face
with my delightful constant companion, Jesus Christ.

And when I'm sure I just can't do anymore,
He just smiles and says . . . "Pedal."

—Author Unknown[1]

Where are you on this bike ride? Are you still in the process of living your boring and predictable life? Are you just climbing aboard the bike? Or have you already begun to pedal? Possibly you're out there in front, pedaling madly, still feeling that you're in control, and asking the Lord to pitch in and help you from the backseat.

Wherever you find yourself today on the Christian journey, know this: If you haven't yet, sooner or later you will find yourself at a point of choosing—choosing whether to let go of the handlebars and let Jesus start navigating from the front seat of the bike. It is at this point of letting go, where belief becomes surrender, that we begin to see our prayers answered and our lives changed.

Richard Foster uses a different metaphor for surrender in his book *Prayer: Finding the Heart's True Home.* He defines it as "a grace-filled releasing of our will and a flowing into the will of the Father."[2]

Deciding to get drenched in the adventure of God's will—clothes, shoes, hairdo, and all—is what surrender is all about. There is a childlike abandon obvious in our lives when we manage to let go and fall into his will. Soaked completely in his Spirit, we find the following prayer for ourselves and each other bubbling up out of the deep places of our spirits:

> May all your expectations be frustrated. May all your plans be thwarted. May all your desires be withered into nothingness. So may you experience the powerlessness and poverty of a child and sing and dance in the mystery of God.[3]

Surrendering Our Idols

A second point of surrender comes as we choose to let go of our idols, our "other gods." This is the essence of the "first and greatest commandment," which tells us we are to love the one true God and him only. (See Matt. 22:36–37 and Exod. 20:2–6.)

Idols, or other gods, come in many sizes and disguises. My husband, Spike, and I were surprised last fall, during a trip to San Francisco, to walk out into the crisp beauty of the September morning and notice that the shop across the street from our hotel sold reproductions of "gods" from every culture and age. You could get Greek gods, like Zeus and his friends, and Native American totem poles as well as New Age crystals "guaranteed" to put you in touch with more modern spirits. We were somewhat appalled to read the sign over the door of this "spiritual boutique." It said (I kid you not), "Gods Are Us!"

But most of our idols are not purchased in stores. They usually come into our lives through more subtle doors. They are the ideas and activities and people that pull us from God's best. They demand our time, attention, money, and spiritual focus, thereby keeping us sidetracked and off-target. And if followed freely, these idols will, in time, consume us.

Idols are often "wants" that we have come to view as "needs" in our lives. Eve wanted a taste of the apple, and when she convinced herself she needed it, she took one. David wanted to "get acquainted" with Bathsheba, and after allowing that *want* to became a *need,* he did. When we allow ourselves to get fixed, focused, even obsessed with those things or people we have our hearts set on, we are creating idols in our lives.

Turning wants into needs is the most common form of modern-day idolatry. It creates an addictive, obsessive lifestyle that views God as incapable of meeting needs and exalts some God-substitute in his place. It says that I must have this other person, this substance, this new car to feed my inner craving, to take care of my inner restlessness, to fill my emptiness of spirit, which only God was meant to fill.

Almost anything, when put in the place of God, can become an idol. As a high school sophomore attending a boarding school for girls in Vicksburg, Mississippi, I got caught up in this kind of unconscious idolatry. Away from home for the first time and terribly homesick for family and friends, I learned to look forward to the comfort of the large, home-cooked meals we were served. Every meal, rich with smooth gravies and creamy deserts, felt like an embrace! There was more comfort available after study hall in the evenings when the canteen opened. I was always in line for something sweet.

I realize now that I was looking to food instead of to God to meet my needs. This kind of idolatry is very subtle and very difficult to put behind you. Even now as an adult, when I am lonely, anxious, or bored, instead of looking to God, at times I find myself tempted to grab some food as a quick fix for whatever's ailing me.

When I feel the pull of that old idol, my best defense is to slow down. If I can postpone an immediate, knee-jerk reaction to "go for the grub," God will strengthen me. If I turn my eyes away from that puny little calorie god to the one, true God, I will find myself able to take my thoughts captive to Christ. Then the Lord will show me what my real need is and begin to meet that need out of the store-house of his perfect will for me.

Whatever your idols are, if your heart's desire is to give them up, God will help you do just that. Philippians 2:13 says that "God is working in you to help you want to do and be able to do what pleases him." This means that even if you're having trouble wanting to surrender, he is at work inside of you, helping you want what he wants. That's good news!

Surrendering Our Losses

One ongoing area of surrender in every life is the surrender of life's inevitable losses. Some losses are large. Some are small. None is easy. Loss can enter our lives in big, dramatic ways like death or divorce. Or it can come in everyday ways: We grow older, we change, loved ones move away.

No one is exempt from these difficult and unwanted actualities. So how do we deal with the pain of loss? Where do we go with our confusion, our outrage, our grief?

I have been contending with a small loss this year that has to do with my body. Though I have never been a serious athlete, I enjoy jogging every day and have entered a number of amateur road races over the years. When I first began running more than fifteen years ago, I could knock off a 10-kilometer (6.2-mile) race in around fifty-four minutes. These days the exact same distance is more difficult and takes much longer. This is a minimal loss, to be sure, but I hate the fact that I have slowed down. I even hate recording it in this book! It signifies to me that I am growing older.

But the Lord has been showing me a way of surrendering this loss to him. When I feel the sting of growing older, I stop and surrender all the decades of my life to him.

"Lord," I say, "I give you my fifties, my sixties, my seventies, my eighties, my nineties. However many years you desire to give me, I give back to you. You already know the number of my days (see Ps. 139:16). They were a gift, and I now return them to you. I surrender all the changes and losses that will come with these years as well as all the joys and the celebrations, for I know you to be a God of love, and I can trust you with them."

A sweet peace comes to me when I surrender this area of loss to God and feel him take hold. The sting goes out of letting go.

But not all losses are as gradual and natural as growing older. Some are brutal, and their effects, devastating. I recently had a long visit with a friend I'll call Amy, who shared with me the details of a tremendous loss in her life that happened many years ago.

When Amy was in her teens, she got pregnant by a young man whom she loved and hoped to marry. But when her parents found out about the pregnancy, they made what they thought was a wise decision. They decided that Amy should have an abortion. That abortion was the most devastating event in Amy's life, one that she had never fully dealt with or gotten over, though she is now in her early fifties.

Then one day not long ago, reading the paper, Amy saw an ad for a weekend retreat designed to help women deal with the emotional after-effects of abortion. Somewhat tentatively, she filled out the form and sent in her money, wondering how much help she could possibly get for a wound that was more than thirty-five years old.

As it turned out, that weekend was truly life-changing for my friend. Amy was able to forgive her parents for what she considered a cruel and heartless decision. She was able to receive forgiveness and grace from God for the guilt and shame that she had carried for more than three decades. She found love and acceptance in the eyes and the stories of the other women whose pain was so similar to her own.

Most importantly, though, she was able to surrender her baby boy into God's arms in a beautiful, symbolic way. The women were encouraged to give names to their unborn children and to choose some memorial act that would commemorate the little life that had been lost. Amy chose to name her unborn son "William" after his father. The week after the retreat, she had a small brass plaque engraved with these words:

To William, my precious son. I loved you,
and I loved your father, Mom.

Then she sent the plaque to be mounted on the Wall of the Unborn in memory of her child.

Amy said that as she mailed the little plaque at the post office, she experienced a tremendous healing. She could see herself handing back to God the gift of William as well as all the pain connected with his conception and his death. She felt a peaceful release in the realization that God will be holding baby William until she meets him in heaven someday.

Surrendering the Past and the Future

We cannot be fully surrendered to God until we have let him have both the past and the future. In Matthew 6:34, Jesus cautions his followers to face the fact that they are time-bound. He encourages them to embrace this day, this hour, this minute because "each day has enough trouble of its own."

The words of our Lord contain, as always, wisdom for our own age. They are no less true today than they were then. A look at our own century reveals advancements in many areas. We've split atoms, forged into space, and found cures for diseases. But no one has ever discovered how to live more than one minute at a time.

We are creatures of time, created to dwell in the present moment, and yet I know hardly a person who is able to accomplish that feat with much serenity. We are constantly straining at the seams of our confinement, trying to push out into the future or back into the past.

We are either looking back at the "good old days" or regretting what was or might have been. We are either looking forward in dread of what awful thing might happen or looking forward in anticipation of the great day when "our ship finally comes in." Either way—whether we are looking backward or forward—we are robbing ourselves of the only moment we can ever truly inhabit.

The best way to embrace our time-bound status is to surrender our yesterdays and our tomorrows to God, to freely put into his hands what is already there anyway—time! When we do that, we will know the freedom of living simply in the now. Then, perhaps, we will find ourselves able to share the rejoicing of Abraham Joshua Heschel, who said, "Who is worthy to be present at the constant unfolding of time? Amidst the meditation of mountains, the humility of flowers—clouds that die constantly for the sake of His glory. . . . Only one response can maintain us: gratefulness for witnessing the wonder."[4]

What greater wisdom than to live surrendered to God in the present moment, witnessing the wonder of "the constant unfolding" of today rather than mentally thrashing about in those worlds we can never physically inhabit anyway—the past and the future.

Surrendering Our Things

Recently I told Spike that I know what I want on my tombstone. I want it to bear the words, "It was all GRACE," for the longer I live the more I realize that every good thing in our lives is just the fall-out of God's grace.

It's easier, though, to see some things as gracious gifts than others.

Our children, for instance, we can see as God's creations. Our talents we can see as part of the unique package God gifted us with. But when it comes to the money we earn, we have a tendency to view it as something we earned on our own. It's so much easier to think of financial and material resources as rightfully ours to control, and that makes them harder to surrender.

Francis of Assisi, the thirteenth-century monk who led his "Little Brothers" on a journey of simplicity, found the easiest way to stay detached from the material things of the world was to have no contact with those things at all. He encouraged his joyful band of followers to dress only in "castoffs" and to handle no money whatsoever.[5]

Few, if any, of us will be able to have that kind of physical detachment from possessions and money in this world. But when we allow God's Spirit to break the yoke of "the tyranny of things," we find the spiritual detachment that leads to true freedom. This yoke is broken, "not by fighting but by surrendering," not on the battleground but on our knees.

A. W. Tozer's prayer of surrender is a powerful place to begin:

> Father, I want to know Thee, but my coward heart fears to give up its toys. I cannot part with them without inward bleeding, and I do not try to hide from Thee the terror of the parting. I come trembling, but I do come. Please root from my heart all those things . . . which have become a part of my living self, so that Thou mayest enter and dwell there without a rival.[6]

Surrendering Our Control Over Others

When Spike and I married, I had a fairy-tale notion that life would be idyllic—our relationship, deeply romantic; our children, paragons of perfection. That notion was short lived, for though we have had a very good life together, we have faced many surprises and challenges.

One big surprise for me was to discover that my two sons, Curtis and Andy, were not little robots that I could raise by remote control. Each of them arrived with a mind of his own. Each one was equipped with a God-given free will to make choices—even destructive ones.

It was when the boys were toddlers that I enrolled in the school of "Who's in control here?" I thought I was. After all, I was the cook, so I could choose what food was set on the table. But I discovered that only my children could decide what they would chew and swallow. I could nag them to "eat their green beans" until I was blue in the face, but I couldn't force the food down their throats.

When Andy was in high school, the issue became more serious than green beans. His free will to experiment and choose led him into what became a serious alcohol and drug problem.

During those heartbreaking years, I moved from the kind of prayer that was really just nagging God or worrying in his presence to the kind of prayer that admitted my powerlessness and put Andy and his addiction into God's hands.

But it was a surrender I had to make again and again. Even after God had worked miracles in Andy's life, after he was out of treatment, clean and sober, walking in a new relationship with the Lord, I would find myself worrying and trying to be in control again. That was when I discovered a tool I called my "God Box."

My God Box is a shoebox with a slit in it. During bouts of momentary panic, I would write Andy's name, the date, and the situation I was fretting about on a slip of paper. I would then commit all of it to God by folding the paper and slipping it into the God Box. It was a tangible, visible "sacrament" of surrender, a way of putting it all into God's hands.

Though I am much improved in my need to control the people in my life, I have not totally outgrown my need for the "God Box." When I really feel myself being strangled by that old urge to butt in, I know where to go. At the top of my closet, between my scrapbooks and my hiking boots, it waits. A colorful shoebox full of little folded slips of compulsiveness, each reading, "Your will, not mine."

Surrendering the "Half-Life"

The life of surrender calls us to "let go," not only in the big, dramatic trials and tragedies, but also in the restless, petty preoccupations and the mindless busyness that steal our joy.

Tilden H. Edwards, in his book *Living Simply Through the Day,* describes the restlessness of the unsurrendered soul who stays with surface trivialities rather than risking the depth of spiritual surrender. He avoids the "bits and pieces of the day" that "rush through his mind" when he watches TV or eats too much or buries himself in work. The food, the TV, or the work makes him feel in control: "at least he's doing something—anything." But in the end he has only anesthetized his anxiety and is left dreaming troubled dreams.

Tilden contends that this type of "underlife" is what causes us to cry out like the psalmist, "How long, O Lord? How long must I

tromp through this dense jungle half crazed and blind before the clearing appears?"[7]

The clearing we seek in the daily jungle of our lives is spiritual surrender. Those who never fully surrender live an impoverished version of what is possible. On some level, they know there must be more, but they settle instead for a safe walk, a half-life.

Christians who have known the joy of the surrendered life (even if only in temporary fits and starts) are able to see that it is the only real life and will never be content with less.

THE REAL HERO

Last year in a large, light-filled sanctuary in Mobile, Alabama, I joined hundreds of Christians from many different denominations to hear author-speaker Henri Nouwen share some of the pearls of his journey. The love of the Lord seemed to spill out of this wiry, bespeckled man as he shared in a thick, Dutch accent his anecdotes and insights, enthusiastically gesturing with widespread hands.

One of Nouwen's anecdotes especially spoke to me of spiritual surrender. He told of the day he took his eighty-eight-year-old father to the circus in Germany. Though the circus tent was crowded with wild and colorful sights, Henri was bored—until the trapeze artists came out. Watching their aerial gymnastics, he sat spellbound.

"Now I see what my true vocation should have been," he said to his father.

At the intermission, Henri decided to go over and talk to the trapeze artists. His enthusiastic appreciation of their skill led them to invite him to their practice the next day and to dinner the next night, and soon it was decided that Nouwen would spend his whole vacation traveling with them all over Germany.

One evening during those weeks of travel, Henri sat in the caravan talking to the head of the family of trapeze artists.

"You know," the seasoned performer told Henri, "since I am the main flyer in the act and I can do triples, I get all the applause. But I'll tell you a secret, Henri. I am not the real hero. The real hero is the catcher. One of the greatest mistakes I can make in the air is to try to catch the catcher. If I move my arms around and try to grab for him, we'll miss the catch or break each other's wrists. I just have to make my triple and go down with my eyes closed and my arms out, trusting that the catcher will catch me. And when I'm calm and waiting, he always does."

As Nouwen pointed out that night, we are called upon to do many "triples" in our daily lives. But we are not the heroes. God is the real Hero, for he is the catcher. As we surrender to him, we learn to close our eyes and put out our arms and pray trustingly as Jesus did on Calvary, "Into your hands, O Father, I commit my spirit." This is the joy and the freedom of living the surrendered life.

LET HIM HAVE YOUR LIFE: 1
COME AND SURRENDER

Read and reflect on these verses of Scripture
and the letter from your Abba that follows.

I came to give life—life in all its fullness. JOHN 10:10

Dearest Child,

My Son, Jesus, came into the world so that you could know the complete freedom of living as my child. He came so that you could share an intimate relationship with himself, with me, and with my Holy Spirit. He is offering you "life in all its fullness." But first you must let go of the "half-life" you have been settling for. Let go of despair and take hold of hope. Let go of fear and take hold of love. Let go of your old destination and take hold of this new adventure in him. There is no time like today. Confess your sin and turn from it. Invite him in as Lord and Savior and embark on the journey of a lifetime.

Come and surrender!
Abba

WRITE A LETTER TO YOUR ABBA: 1

PRAYERS OF SURRENDER

*After reading and reflecting on God's words to you,
write your own letter to him, using the following guide:*

1. In your journal or in the space below, respond to the letter you have just read. Will you let go of the things God is asking you to let go of and take hold of the things he is asking you to take hold of? Will you accept his invitation to live "life in all its fullness"?

Dear Abba,

2. Now put down your pen. Ask Abba to speak to you. Sit quietly for ten minutes (or more) and listen to him in your heart. What is he saying to you about a relationship with him? What personal words of love, guidance, or challenge do you hear? Write these out in your journal. (Remember, God's word in your heart will never conflict with his revealed Word in the Bible.) If you choose to make a complete surrender of your life to the Lord for the first time, pray this prayer (or one like it) from your heart:

CLOSING PRAYER: *Dear Jesus, I believe you are the Christ, the Son of the Living God who was crucified and raised again for sinners. I confess to you that I am a sinner in need of a Savior. I bring my sin before you—my pride, my dishonesty, my selfishness—everything that keeps me separated from you, and I ask you to forgive me and save me. I invite you into my heart to be my personal Lord and Savior. Come take control of my life. I pray in your name. Amen.*

LET HIM HAVE YOUR LIFE: 2

LET GO AND LET ME TAKE OVER

Be still, and know that I am God;
I will be exalted among the nations,
I will be exalted in the earth. Ps. 46:10 NIV

My Child,

I see how hard you strive to be a good person, but I long for you to know the joy of letting go. Striving as you do is going at it from the wrong direction. It is using external, fleshly efforts to produce internal, spiritual results. I am your internal source of power. When you live and move and have your being in me, life is so much simpler. The changes you yearn for will flow out of your relationship with me. When you let go and give my Spirit permission to take charge, there is freedom and peace and joy on the journey. Cease striving and know me, for I am the One whose hand is on your life. I am the One whose mercy turns your planet. I am the One who yearns to set you free.

Be still and know that I am God,
Abba

WRITE A LETTER TO YOUR ABBA: 2

PRAYERS OF SURRENDER

1. In your letter to Abba God, tell him whether you have felt "cared for" or whether you have felt a need to strive for results in your life. Choose one area of striving and tell God in writing that you are going to let him be in control of that area this week. See him taking control of it, and describe the difference it will make in your life.

Dear Abba,

_____

_____

_____

_____

_____

_____

_____

2. Now put down your pen. Ask Abba God to speak to you. Remain still and listening for ten minutes (or more). What is he saying in his still, small voice about your attitude of striving? What personal words of love, guidance, or challenge do you hear? Write these out in your journal. (Remember, God's word in your heart will never conflict with his revealed Word in the Bible.)

CLOSING PRAYER: *Dear Abba, I sometimes find it difficult just to relax and trust that I myself am enough to bring into a relationship. Forgive me when I try to earn your love. Forgive me when I try to work out everything in my own strength. Teach me to surrender, Father. Amen.*

LET HIM HAVE YOUR LIFE: 3

TRUST ME WITH TOMORROW

Some of you say, "Today or tomorrow we will go to some city. We will stay there a year, do business, and make money." But you do not know what will happen tomorrow! Your life is like a mist. You can see it for a short time, but then it goes away. So you should say, "If the Lord wants, we will live and do this or that." JAMES 4:13–15

> Plant early in the morning,
>   and work until evening,
> because you don't know if this or that will succeed.
>   ECCLES. 11:6

My Child,

Have you laid careful plans for your future? Have you decided what work you will do and calculated what the result of that work will be? Don't you know that you can plan your work and do it, but you cannot plan the results of that work? The farmer plants his crop, but I bring forth the harvest. You do your work, but I bring forth the results. The sun and rain and climate are in my hands, and so are the circumstances that affect your work. Your only certainty is me. I am the One who holds tomorrow firmly in my hands, and this I say to you: At each turn seek my guidance, and I will instruct you in all your decisions. Enjoy your work. Labor with enthusiasm. Be honest in your dealings and do not compromise. But leave the results of your labor with me.

> *Trust me with tomorrow,*
> *Abba*

WRITE A LETTER TO YOUR ABBA: 3

PRAYERS OF SURRENDER

1. If you knew for certain that you had only one year left to live, what would you do now that you are not doing? Make a small altar out of a tabletop or counter. On it place your calendar, your "Day-Timer," your alarm clock, and your watch. How big a part do these things play in your life? Who owns your seconds, minutes, hours, days, years? If you can honestly do so, write out a prayer of surrender in your journal, putting all of these things in God's hands.

Dear Abba,

2. Now put down your pen. Ask Abba to speak to you. Sit quietly for ten minutes (or more) and listen to him in your heart. What is he saying to you about his ownership of tomorrow? What personal words of love, guidance, or challenge do you hear? Write these out in your journal. (Remember, God's word in your heart will never conflict with his revealed Word in the Bible.)

CLOSING PRAYER: *Dear Abba, I confess to you that I am constantly trying to control my time without asking you how I should spend it. And I also confess that there are moments and days when time takes control of me. I choose today to put my tomorrows in your hands. Show me how to spend the moments so that my life will line up with your will for me. Amen.*

LET HIM HAVE YOUR LIFE: 4

DON'T WAIT TO SURRENDER

To be spiritually minded is life and peace. ROM. 8:6 KJV

Thou wilt keep him in perfect peace, whose mind is stayed on thee: because he trusteth in thee. ISA. 26:3 KJV

I have told you these things, so that in me you may have peace. In this world you will have trouble. But take heart! I have overcome the world. JOHN 16:33 NIV

Dearest Child,

Don't wait until your life is well ordered and organized before you surrender it to me. If you wait, you may never come at all! The order and peace you seek is in me. Surrendering to me will bring that inner serenity you have yearned for, rearranging your heart into a dwelling of comfort and beauty where my Holy Spirit can abide. And when you have given my Son his rightful place in your inner life, your outer circumstances lose their power to bully and harass you. So come. Leave the world's frantic pace. Enter into this new relationship. Drink deeply of my peace and learn to live as my child.

Lovingly,
Abba

WRITE A LETTER TO YOUR ABBA: 4

PRAYERS OF SURRENDER

1. Are you trying to create peace and order in your life while you put off your relationship with God until you "get things organized"? If so, confess this in your letter to Abba God today. Acknowledge that your peace is in him. Write this out in your prayer: "Abba, strengthen me to surrender to you so that I may know your peace."

Dear Abba,

_____

_____

_____

_____

_____

_____

_____

_____

_____

2. Now put down your pen. Ask Abba to speak to you. Sit quietly for ten minutes (or more) and listen to him in your heart. What is he saying to you about your Source of peace? What personal words of love, guidance, or challenge do you hear? Write these out in your journal. (Remember, God's word in your heart will never conflict with his revealed Word in the Bible.)

CLOSING PRAYER: *Dear Abba, I need your peace today. I come to you seeking your order and your serenity. Give me the grace to let you take over in my heart. In Jesus' name, Amen.*

LET HIM HAVE YOUR LIFE: 5

YOU CAN BE A SPIRIT-WALKER

There is therefore now no condemnation for those who are in Christ Jesus. . . . For the law of the Spirit of life in Christ Jesus has made me free from the law of sin and death. ROM. 8:1–2 NKJV

Child of Mine,

I see your struggle. So many mornings you unconsciously, automatically slide into that worn and familiar groove of the flesh-walker, ignoring your spirit-self. No wonder you find yourself feeling weary, unworthy, and unable to live up to all that's expected of you. I have a new life for you. But you will never take hold of it until you let go of self-condemnation. You must learn to walk in my Spirit of freedom. Where can you learn this? If "walking in the Spirit" were an Olympic event, you would train for it in the gymnasium of surrender. Faithful surrender is very different from fatalistic giving up. It is actively choosing to believe. It is taking faith in hand and plugging it into the reality of Jesus Christ. Once you have made him your Lord and your Savior, you have the power to live as a Spirit-walker, for my Spirit power will flow through you, bringing strength for every challenge. So, each morning be filled afresh with my Spirit. Lift your heart to Jesus. Set your mind on "Spirit things." And you will know the freedom of the Spirit walk.

Powerfully,
Abba

WRITE A LETTER TO YOUR ABBA: 5
PRAYERS OF SURRENDER

1. In your letter to Abba God, tell him what "walking in the Spirit" means to you. The Holy Spirit is described in the New Testament as a teacher, counselor, guide, strengthener, friend. Which of those qualities are important to you now? Tell the Father how the Holy Spirit could make a difference in your life in one or more of those roles.

Dear Abba,

_____

_____

_____

_____

_____

_____

_____

_____

2. Now put down your pen. Ask Abba to speak to you. Sit quietly for ten minutes (or more) and listen to him in your heart. What is he saying to you about walking in the Spirit? What personal words of love, guidance, or challenge do you hear? Write these out in your journal. (Remember, God's word in your heart will never conflict with his revealed Word in the Bible.)

CLOSING PRAYER: *Dear Abba, thank you for making it possible for me to live a Spirit-empowered life. I choose to plug my faith into the reality of Jesus Christ so that I can fully know and share the power of his Spirit. Teach me to be a Spirit-walker. In Jesus' name. Amen.*

CHAPTER THREE

WORSHIP WITH YOUR WHOLE HEART

WORSHIP WITH YOUR
WHOLE HEART

I once wrote a parable called "The Cloak of Miracles" in which a small, tattered girl travels a steep road to a distant city. After facing and overcoming many perils, with the help of friends along the way she finally arrives at her destination:

> The girl stood alone now facing the glorious gate. . . .
> Summoning all of her courage, she lifted the golden latch, and
> as she did, slowly, silently, the great gate swung open before her.
> Stepping inside and looking around, her eyes widened, for she
> gazed into the wonder of a land unlike any she had ever known.
> A soft, glowing halo of light hung in the air, and a sweet fra-
> grance clung to everything.
>
> "How beautiful!" whispered the girl. "Oh, how very beautiful!"
>
> "So you are here at last," said a familiar voice behind her. She
> turned and found herself looking into the kindest eyes she had
> ever seen. Gentle eyes of warmth and compassion.
>
> "You are Home, my daughter," said the Lover of Souls in

the same deep, kind voice she had heard many times in her heart. . . .

The small girl's heart was flooded with joy as she stood now with the Lover of Souls, surrounded by the sights and sounds of the city that was distant no longer. . . . She was warm and safe and filled with more joy than her small heart could contain. For her tears had been dried, her questions had been answered, and her heart had reached its destination.

If you knew of a road that would lead to a city where your heavenly Father made his home, would you take that road? If you were confident that at the end of that road there would be a gate opening into a beautiful land where you would be in his presence and experience his love in person, would you walk through that open gate?

Well, there is such a road, and we have been invited to travel it. There is such a gate, and we have been invited to enter it.

> Come into his city with songs of thanksgiving
> and into his courtyards with songs of praise.
> Thank him and praise his name. (Ps. 100:4)

THE ROAD OF WORSHIP

The road we travel is paved with praise. The gate we step through is hinged with thanksgiving. Our way into the Father's presence is the way of worship. As we come through the gate and into his courts, we take a deep breath and find ourselves flooded with new life, for we are breathing the spiritual oxygen for which we were created, standing in the spiritual climate for which we were designed.

Worship puts us in God's presence, whether we are in a room crowded with other believers or walking alone on a tranquil beach, lifting unspoken love to the God of all creation, for both corporate and personal worship set us in right relationship with God. Both place him above us as the gracious Giver of all things and ourselves bowed in adoration before him as his children.

But because the journey we have embarked on in this book is one of personal prayer, we will be focusing primarily on personal worship. Nothing is more important in forming a friendship with the Father than spending time alone in his presence, worshiping him, and yet many of us shortchange ourselves (and God) in this area.

Perhaps that is true because we feel we don't quite know how to worship him in private. We have been given little instruction in this spiritual discipline. We cannot spy on another person's private time with the Lord, so we have no model. Or we may feel slightly intimidated by what we see as the "mechanics" of personal worship. Singing out loud to the Father, for instance, in a room all by ourselves may make us feel inhibited. Or perhaps we don't understand the benefit of worship. What does God get out of it? What do we? All of these questions are worth exploring as we look at the beautiful gift, the exciting adventure of personal worship.

WHERE WORSHIP BEGINS

Probably the first question worth asking about worship is: "Where does it begin?" Do we just wake up one day with a desire to fall on our faces before God in praise? No. The human heart, apart from God's wooing, is not inclined to turn to him.

Jesus said, "No one can come to me unless the Father draws him to me" (John 6:44). We are drawn to worship by the One we worship. Or, as Richard Foster puts it in his book, *Celebration of Discipline,* "Worship is the human response to the divine initiative."[1]

When Jesus spoke to the Samaritan woman at the well, he revealed his Father's fervent, personal search for those who will worship him "in spirit and in truth." God is on a mission—a quest. He is looking for worshipers. As he constantly draws each of us into a deeper and more intimate friendship with himself, he is creating within us hearts that will praise him. So, lest we feel somehow holier than others when we are caught up in a moment of worship, we had best remember that we can't even praise him apart from his initiative and power!

THE LESSON OF A LYRIC

I remember that revelation being brought home to me at a lyric-writing seminar in the Rocky Mountains one summer. Our homework was to bring in a completed worship lyric the next morning.

I was not daunted by the prospect of writing a lyric in one day. In fact, I was so undaunted that I put it off until about thirty minutes before class the next morning.

Then in a panic I said this pathetically pragmatic prayer: "Oh, God! I've got to have a lyric in thirty minutes. Help me! Show me something about worship so I can put it into a lyric."

Suddenly I began to laugh. "Lord," I said, "forgive me. I see how dependent I am on you for everything—even the words I need to praise you!"

I wrote this lyric that morning. (Lynn Keesecker and I later turned it into a song recorded by the Imperials.)

> Even the praise comes from you;
> Every song that I raise comes from you.
> Fill my mouth with words of worship,
> And I'll give them back to you
> 'Cause even the praise,
> Every feeling and phrase,
> Even the praise comes from you.[2]

HIS LEAD, OUR RESPONSE

God is waiting anxiously to lead each of us in the dance of praise. Just as I used to stand on my daddy's shoes as a little girl and let him lead me in a waltz around the room, our heavenly Abba will take the leading role in the worship experience. Our part is to follow his lead—to respond to his initiative.

Often on busy days I'm not very responsive. I forget to worship. I move into my "achievement mode" of "getting things done." So many responsibilities call to me in insistent voices: "Do me! Take care of me! Turn your attention here!" In contrast, God's invitation to worship is delivered in a "still, small voice" that can easily be drowned out if my heart is not kept in a state of readiness.

The more I learn about worship, the more I realize that whatever is on the "to do" agenda will flow more smoothly when my day is first grounded in praise. The more I have to face on any given day, the more I need it.

Once when I was under the pressure of a writing deadline, my friend Pam told me, "Claire, invest your prime time before the Lord, and he'll get you through the rest of it. Pray for two hours. Write for one. That's a good ratio."

Pam's praise prescription seemed overly idealistic to me at the time, but I have found that the closer I come to following it, the better my work goes. The work flows from the praise. The doing flows from the being.

Oswald Chambers said that the lasting value of what we do for God "is measured by the depth of the intimacy of our private times of fellowship and oneness with Him. Rushing in and out of worship is wrong every time—there is always plenty of time to worship God."[3]

CREATIVE WAYS AROUND OUR ROADBLOCKS

I know, I know. You are probably thinking that Oswald may have had plenty of time to worship God, but you don't. In the rush and busyness of your daily life, there is not plenty of time for anything, much less sitting alone focusing on God's goodness while the dirty dishes, dirty clothes, and dirty children seem to multiply around you.

But I truly believe that if you will ask God to make a space for worship in your day, he will answer that prayer. I believe that because I know it is his will that you worship him, and he will move heaven and earth to bring about his will in us when we desire it.

Our friend Lisa Yearwood, the busy mother of three daughters, is unable to find a large block of daily time to worship God, so she finds mini-worship times throughout the day. Waiting in the car to pick up carpool kids, folding clothes, or doing any basically "mindless" task can be a small occasion of praise.

God also provided my friend Signa with a creative solution to her personal time crunch. Signa's unconventional working hours as a caterer had been draining her energy and robbing her of time with the Lord and her family. As she and her husband, Conlee, sought God's guidance for an answer to this dilemma, the Lord provided a thoroughly unique plan.

"Begin your day at sunset rather than at sunrise," he instructed, "as was the custom of My people for generations. At the 'beginning' of your day, read My Word that I have given you, speak to Me from your heart, and then listen. Allow Me to prepare you for the rest you need to begin the next morning with Me."

On weekdays both Signa and Conlee "began their day" at sunset, reading Scripture, sharing, listening for God's word, praying for each other and their children. Then they would go to bed early, content that they had begun their day together in the evening rather than starting out in an early morning climate of stress and hurry.

The next morning at 5 A.M. Signa would find herself joyously engaged in personal worship as she drove through dark city streets on the way to work, and later as she would worshipfully watch the sun rise over the Celtic cross of a nearby church. On God's new schedule of work and worship, Signa was amazed at the renewed energy and refreshed attitude God was pouring out into every area of her life.[4]

WHAT WE GIVE, NOT WHAT WE GET

Renewed energy and a refreshed attitude are among many benefits we may derive from personal worship, but rather than being based on what we can get from God, our motivation for worship must always be based on a desire to give to him.

As Merlin Carothers put it in his book *Power in Praise,* "Praise is not a bargaining position. We don't say, 'I'll praise you so that you can bless me, Lord.' . . . Praise is based on a total and joyful acceptance of the present . . . not on what we think or hope will happen in the future."[5]

The psalmist did not say in Psalm 37:4, "Delight yourself in the LORD *so that he will give you* the desires of your heart." He said, "Delight yourself in the LORD *and he will give you* the desires of your heart" (NIV). God's blessings often follow praise but not because we have been able to manipulate him.

I have found in my own life that his blessings come to me as my heart is changed by worship. As I honor him with my gift of worship, my desires for myself begin to line up with his desires for me, and then he is pleased to grant them!

WORSHIP FOR EVERY OCCASION

How do we bring the gift of worship that truly honors him? It isn't a secret spiritual formula known by a select few. It doesn't take a harp or a lyre. We don't have to be eloquent or talented. Praise should be as natural as breathing.

In a recent conference on spiritual warfare, Bible teacher Alice Smith revealed the appealing simplicity of the way she worships.

"First," she said, "before I read a word in the Bible or tell him about a single concern, I just 'brag on him' for forty-five minutes. I look around at his creation and tell him what a good job he did on it. I think of all the good things in the world and in my life and I compliment him on his wisdom and generosity. There's not a man alive who doesn't like to be bragged on!" The simple gratitude and humility of Alice's prayer is the key to genuine worship.

But I must confess that there are days when my circumstances don't seem to lend themselves to worship. Days when I do not feel humble or grateful. Days when I feel so caught in my own problems or so pulled down by my own depression that entering into worship would almost feel hypocritical. What am I to do on those days?

You guessed it. On those days I am to worship anyway! I am to bring the Lord what the Bible calls sacrificial praise: "So through Jesus let us always offer to God our sacrifice of praise, coming from lips that speak his name" (Heb. 13:15).

Worship is for difficult and dark times as well as for joyful ones. When we acknowledge God's sovereignty even in a pit of darkness, even in the desert of our emotions, we introduce the light of his love into the darkness of our situation.

I will never forget this being demonstrated to me at a time of severe grief. My friend Himmie and I were praying with another friend, Melissa, after the tragic death of Melissa's son, Zeb. We began by drawing near to God and asking him to comfort and console Melissa and her other children. Then, somewhere in the middle of those quiet petitions, Himmie lifted her beautiful soprano voice and began to sing, "We Bring the Sacrifice of Praise."

"I didn't feel joyful at all," she explained to Melissa and me later. "I just felt led to praise God right then as a way of acknowledging his Lordship over everything that has happened and everything that is to come."

INSTRUCTING TRAINABLE SPIRITS

It's far more difficult to praise God in dark times, but it is something we can learn to do. Just as our parents taught us those little acts of kindness and gratitude that we call "good manners," we can teach our spirits to worship. They may be slow learners, but they are trainable!

David, the Old Testament expert on praise, was instructing himself in the act of worship when he said in Psalm 103:

> My whole being, praise the LORD;
>   all my being, praise his holy name.

If we're willing to learn from them, our problems can often be excellent teachers in the school of praise. Our friend Phillip suffered severe financial setbacks in the recession of the early 1980s, but what he gained was a heart of gratitude. Spike and I are always brought to tears by the spontaneous prayers that spring from Phillip's childlike spirit. When thanking God, he takes nothing for granted.

"O God, thank you for food to eat," he will say. "Thank you for clothes to wear, homes to live in, work to do." How those expressions of praise must please his heavenly Father!

Like Phillip, each of us can cultivate a heart of gratitude as we look back through our lives and relive our personal encounters with the living God.

A CELEBRATION OR A QUIET REFLECTION

Once our gratitude has cleared a path into God's presence, how do we express ourselves? God created us with so many personal facets, so many feelings and emotions, all of which "are a legitimate part of the human personality and should be employed in worship."[6] There are days when we feel joyful, excited, exuberant, and other days when we feel a deep need to "be still, and know that [he is] God" (Ps. 46:10 NIV). Both expressions of worship are valid. As long as we stay tuned in to the Holy Spirit, our heart's response, whatever it is, can be offered up as an act of worship.

An exuberant heart response is almost always a sure thing for me when the first day of real autumn comes to Alabama. After four to five months of intense heat, complete with humidity, yellow flies, and mosquitoes, cool weather is an unbelievable high! Several weeks ago I woke up to such a day. Incredibly clear, blue, totally cloudless sky; monarch butterflies in and out among our many-colored flowers; temperature in the sixties. Glory!

I put on my Dennis Jernigan CD, "Lion of Judah," and I was bouncing around the house singing praises to God before I even stopped to dress or eat breakfast. After an almost aerobic series of praise choruses, I was drawn by the music into the place of God's holiness where I could experience his deep reality. All day long my heart echoed the words of Psalm 16:11 ("In Your presence is fullness of joy" NKJV) as I returned again and again to celebrate my time with him.

Another very different kind of day, sitting all alone on Pam's front porch at Choctaw Bluff with my Bible open in my lap, I had a different kind of worship experience. I had been feeling pretty down on myself for weeks, struggling with a bad case of writer's block. Just the day before I had received in the mail another book written by an extremely prolific author-friend who seems to write ten books to my one! Feeling more like pouting than praying, there was not much worship rising to the surface in my spirit.

Then suddenly my eye was caught by a little spider literally jumping along the painted floorboards of the porch. He seemed so spunky and so pleased with himself! Very near the jumping spider, ambling slowly, one thread-like leg at a time, up one of the white porch columns, was a huge daddy longlegs.

For a long time I just watched those two spiders without thinking anything. The little jumping spider disappeared quickly. The daddy longlegs continued his trek toward the ceiling. As a soft breeze stirred around me, I lifted my eyes. I found myself looking at dozens of different kinds of trees. Oaks. Pines. Pecans. Each variety had a different kind of bark. A different leaf or needle. I was surrounded by a stereophonic symphony of bird songs, and gliding out across the river, like an angel, was a snowy egret.

"Lord, what are you saying to me?" I asked him.

"Claire," I seemed to hear him say, "I delight in the diversity of my creation. In spiders, in trees, in birds, in people. I made you just as you are, and I delight in you just as you are. When you are critical of yourself and impatient with yourself, when you compare yourself with others, you hurt me, for you are criticizing me and my design for your life. Learn to agree with me about who you are. You are my child. You are a priceless work of art!"

I sat very still in his presence then, feeling very much a part of his creation as I let his words sink in. I wrote one sentence in the margin of my Bible that day. It said, "I praise you, for I am your work of art." And though I had not sung a single song or lifted my hands or gotten down on my knees, I knew in my heart that I had worshiped.

A CHANNEL OF POWER

When we worship, when our hearts are kept continually in God's presence, we are opening a channel of power into our circumstances. When we bring our hearts and minds and souls and strength to focus worshipfully on him and his goodness, our praise becomes a catalyst for change. God's power flows through our worship and into our circumstances, altering our lives.

Shortly after our son, Andy, became a Christian (following his senior year in high school) he was admitted to a drug-treatment program where he went into recovery from drug and alcohol addiction.

We were so grateful to God for his mercy and his hand on Andy's life. We were so proud of Andy for his honesty and his desire to change. And yet when Andy came out of treatment, we were aware of what a struggle this new Christian lifestyle was going to be for him initially.

He returned to Mobile a "new creation," but there were parts of his old life that had not changed. One of those was the kind of music he listened to. Many of the singing groups that were his old favorites pushed negative, destructive, even suicidal messages. He realized they were not good for the new journey he was on, and yet he didn't see Christian music as an alternative. That was when his friend David gave him a challenge.

"Do a little experiment with me, Andy," David said, handing him a stack of Christian tapes. "Just listen to these tapes on the way to work and on the way home. The rest of the day you can listen to anything you want. Try it for a month, and just see what happens. I dare you!"

Andy agreed. On the way to his job as a carpenter and on the way home, he would pop in tapes by singers like Wayne Watson and Rich Mullins. In less than a week he could feel a change taking place in his spirit. He began to feel more hopeful and excited about life. As his heart joined in with the message of the music, he would often sing along. Andy even started sharing the tapes and his new-found faith with his coworker, Mike, and before the job was over Mike, too, had given his life to the Lord.

Andy left that job to go to college, and the next job he held was that of youth pastor at our church. Today Andy is a full-time musician who writes and performs his own songs—songs that bring to young listeners the same kind of hope he needed when he was struggling.[7]

Personal worship always funnels God's power into our circumstances. When we learn the daily walk of worship we discover that "it is possible for every motion of our lives to have its root in God."[8]

THE DAILY WALK OF WORSHIP

This daily walk leads us into the presence of the One who loves us. There we offer him our all—our joy, our gratitude, our times of celebration, our conflicts, our questions, and our baffling circumstances—choosing in faith to submerge them in his great ocean of love. This "hidden, personal, worshipping life of a saint" is what Oswald Chambers believed to be the "most essential element" on the Christian journey.[9]

I recently saw my friend Janie, who gave me a glimpse into the heart of a worshiper. A mutual acquaintance had told me that since Janie and her children had moved from Alabama her teenage daughter had been diagnosed with a serious illness. I expected to see the strain in Janie's face, but instead I saw the strength and glow of inner faith.

"How in the world have you held up so well through all of this?" I asked her.

"Claire," she answered smiling, "I have literally stayed on my face before the Lord since the diagnosis."

"Praying for healing?" I asked.

"Some," she answered. "But mostly just worshiping him. That's where my strength and my sanity lie."

Nothing we can do is capable of bringing more strength, more sanity, more hope, more joy to the daily reality of life than worshiping God. Are you walking this daily walk of worship with your Abba? If not, there is no time like today to begin. I challenge you just as Andy's friend David challenged him all those years ago when he shoved a stack of Christian tapes in his hands, saying, "Just try it for a month and see what happens. I dare you!"

WORSHIP WITH YOUR WHOLE HEART: 1

YOU WERE MADE TO WORSHIP ME

*Read and reflect on these verses of Scripture
and the letter from your Abba that follows.*

O LORD, our Lord,
    how majestic is your name in all the earth!
You have set your glory
    above the heavens.
From the lips of children and infants
    you have ordained praise. PS. 8:1–2A NIV

How lovely is your dwelling place,
    O LORD Almighty!
My soul yearns, even faints,
    for the courts of the LORD;
my heart and my flesh cry out
    for the living God. . . .
Blessed are those who dwell in your house;
    they are ever praising you. PS. 84:1, 2, 4 NIV

My Child,

*Know this: You are never more fully who you were meant to be than
when you are worshiping me. It was for worship that you were created. All
vestiges of low self-esteem vanish as you find yourself caught up at last in
the role for which you were designed. The walls within you that segregated
reason from rejoicing, thought from thanksgiving, the cerebral from the
celebratory all come down and you become ONE PERSON, healed and
whole and holy, standing straight up, heart and hands and head uplifted in
the act of being my child. And, oh glory! You are beautiful! Come and be
your real, true self.*

Come and worship,
Abba

WRITE A LETTER TO YOUR ABBA: 1
PRAYERS OF ADORATION

After reading and reflecting on God's words to you,
write your own letter to him, using the following guide:

1. In your journal or in the space below, describe any walls within you
   that you would like to see brought down. Have you thought of your life
   in compartments such as the spiritual part, the career part, the social
   part? In writing, ask God to begin bringing those walls down inside of
   you as you learn to worship him.

   Dear Abba,

   _____

   _____

   _____

   _____

   _____

   _____

2. Now put down your pen. Ask Abba to speak to you. Sit quietly for ten
   minutes (or more) and listen to him in your heart. What is he saying
   to you about worshiping him wholeheartedly? What personal words of
   encouragement, love, guidance, or challenge do you hear? Write these
   out in your journal. (Remember, God's word in your heart will never
   conflict with his revealed Word in the Bible.)

   CLOSING PRAYER: *Dear Abba, thank you for the joy and the*
   privilege of coming into your presence. Thank you for the gift of praise.
   I long to worship you with all that I am. Take my divided heart, O Lord,
   and make it whole. Amen.

WORSHIP WITH YOUR WHOLE HEART: 2

A SMALL KINGDOM

For to us a child is born, to us a son is given, and the government will be on his shoulders. And he will be called Wonderful Counselor, Mighty God, Everlasting Father, Prince of Peace. ISA. 9:6 NIV

> He brought me to the banquet room,
> and his banner over me is love. SONG OF SONGS 2:4

Therefore, as God's chosen people, holy and dearly loved, clothe yourselves with compassion, kindness, humility, gentleness and patience. Bear with each other and forgive whatever grievances you may have against one another. Forgive as the Lord forgave you. And over all these virtues put on love, which binds them all together in perfect unity. Let the peace of Christ rule in your hearts, since as members of one body you were called to peace. And be thankful. COL. 3:12–15 NIV

Dear One,

My spirit within you creates a new order of living. Your heart has become a small kingdom of joy and peace. My Son has ascended the throne as monarch of this kingdom, and he has brought with him a reign of justice and kindness and harmony. Acts of love and deeds of mercy are the hallmark of his reign in this tiny nation of your heart, and the banner that flies above it is love. Gratitude and thankfulness shine here like the sun. Let the song that goes forth from the kingdom of your heart ever be a song of praise and worship!

> *Come rejoicing,*
> *Abba*

WRITE A LETTER TO YOUR ABBA: 2

PRAYERS OF ADORATION

1. In your journal or in the space below, write out a paragraph of praise to Jesus. In the paragraph, proclaim him as King of the kingdom of your heart. Give him reign over all of you. Raise the banner of love over your heart.

Dear Abba,

_____

_____

_____

_____

_____

_____

_____

_____

_____

2. Now put down your pen. Ask Abba to speak to you. Sit quietly for ten minutes (or more) and listen to him in your heart. What is he saying to you about allowing Jesus to reign more fully? What personal words of love, guidance, or challenge do you hear? Write these out in your journal. (Remember, God's word in your heart will never conflict with his revealed Word in the Bible.)

CLOSING PRAYER: *Dear Abba, thank you for sending your Son, Jesus, to be the King of my heart. Forgive me when I take control of things and start going in my own direction. Help me always to remember and welcome his reign in me. I worship you, Abba Father. I yield my life to you and to him. Amen.*

WORSHIP WITH YOUR WHOLE HEART: 3
TO WORSHIP IS TO BE CHANGED

Look to the LORD and his strength; seek his face always. 1 CHRON. 16:11 NIV

When he cries out to me, I will hear, for I am compassionate. EXOD. 22:27 NIV

Worship the LORD with gladness;
    come before him with joyful songs. PS. 100:2 NIV

My Dear Child,

To worship me is to be changed. Changed by the presence of my love and power and mercy. Changed in improbable and lovely and sometimes illogical ways into a person you never imagined you could be. To worship is to believe there is Someone higher, wiser, and more powerful than you who cares and listens and takes joy in you. I am that Someone. To worship is to embrace my healing love and my plans for you, which exceed all that you can imagine or hope for. It is to agree with my sovereign Fatherhood. To worship is to open the pores of your being to me—to come in total honesty, bringing your real self, offering your whole heart. So come often to me, my child. Lift your heart in my presence where I wait for you, and you will be changed into who you were designed to be—into the image of my Son.

Your Father,
Abba

WRITE A LETTER TO YOUR ABBA: 3

PRAYERS OF ADORATION

1. Have you ever "opened the pores of your being" in total transparency to God? Do you realize that he waits for your lifted heart? Write a prayer of worship, praising God for his availability to you, his Father-love for you, his mercy that is healing you, his willingness to change you into the image of his Son.

Dear Abba,

_____

_____

_____

_____

_____

_____

_____

_____

2. Now put down your pen. Ask Abba to speak to you. Sit quietly for ten minutes (or more) and listen to him in your heart. What is he saying to you about being changed by worship? What personal words of encouragement, love, guidance, or challenge do you hear? Write these out in your journal. (Remember, God's word in your heart will never conflict with his revealed Word in the Bible.)

CLOSING PRAYER: *Dear Abba, though change is uncomfortable, I do not want to miss your will for my life. Make me more willing to embrace your changes as I learn to worship you. Make me "moldable" as you have your way in my life. Amen.*

WORSHIP WITH YOUR WHOLE HEART: 4

LET HIS JOY BE IN YOU

As the Father has loved me, so have I loved you. Now remain in my love.
If you obey my commands, you will remain in my love, just as I have obeyed
my Father's commands and remain in his love. I have told you this so that my
joy may be in you and that your joy may be complete. JOHN 15:9–11 NIV

He is your praise; he is your God. DEUT. 10:21A NIV

He put a new song in my mouth,
      a hymn of praise to our God. PS. 40:3A NIV

My Dear Child,

*Do your days seem to go by in shades of gray? Have you misplaced
your heart of wonder? Have you lost your sense of awe? There is joy
waiting for you closer than your heartbeat. Joy that radiates all the colors
of new life. Joy that will well up from within, from the springs of my
Spirit. To find this joy, you must begin to shift the focus of your soul. You
must learn to abide (remain, dwell) in the reality of my love, and when
you do, up from the center of your being will bubble songs of praise, and
words of worship. You must begin to center your heart on the reality of
my Son, and when you do, your soul will be flooded with new sounds
of celebration. Let his joy be in you and your joy will be complete!*

Abide in my Son,
Abba

WRITE A LETTER TO YOUR ABBA: 4

PRAYERS OF ADORATION

1. Tell Abba God in writing about the level of joy in your life right now. Write in your journal or in the space below some ways that you can stay more aware of his nearness tomorrow. Ask him to rekindle joy, awe, and childlike wonder in your heart as you worship him.

Dear Abba,

_____

_____

_____

_____

_____

_____

_____

2. Now put down your pen. Ask Abba to speak to you. Sit quietly for ten minutes (or more) and listen to him in your heart. What is he saying to you about being open to his joy? What personal words of love, guidance, or challenge do you hear? Write these out in your journal. (Remember, God's word in your heart will never conflict with his revealed Word in the Bible.)

CLOSING PRAYER: *Dear Abba, so often my days take on a routine sameness. I forget to worship you in the small, seemingly insignificant times and places. Lord, I miss that childlike heart of wonder and awe. I open my heart to you now in praise and ask you to fill me with your joy. Amen.*

WORSHIP WITH YOUR WHOLE HEART: 5

DRESS YOURSELF IN PRAISE

> I will give them a crown to replace their ashes,
>   and the oil of gladness to replace their sorrow,
>   and clothes of praise to replace their spirit of sadness. Isa. 61:3

My Child,

*I have seen your sadness. I have wept with you in your times of
depression. I have watched you struggle with temptation. Now I long to
replace those threadbare rags of your old life with beautiful garments spun
from the fabric of my Spirit—gleaming white garments of praise. I place
on your head a crown to replace the ashes of your old regrets. I place on
your shoulders a robe of righteousness to replace that shapeless dress of
depression and sadness. I anoint you with the oil of gladness to take away
the musty aroma of gloom. Now, with dry eyes and an expectant heart,
come before me. Glory in my love for you and go forth into your new life,
celebrating the presence of my redeeming mercy.*

> *Your Abba,*
> *God*

WRITE A LETTER TO YOUR ABBA: 5
PRAYERS OF ADORATION

1. In your journal or in the space below, tell Abba God what you will have to set aside to be dressed in his new garments of worship. What rags are you discarding? Are they rags of depression? Fear? Hopelessness? Envy? Bitterness? Unforgiveness? Ask the Lord to show you what they are, and as you take them off, write, "This day [write the date] I am discarding the rags of [write names of the old garments God reveals], and I am putting on his garments of praise."

Dear Abba,

_____

_____

_____

_____

_____

2. Now put down your pen. Ask Abba to speak to you. Sit quietly for ten minutes (or more) and listen to him in your heart. What is he saying to you about wearing these new clothes of worship? What personal words of love, guidance, or challenge do you hear? Write these out in your journal. (Remember, God's word in your heart will never conflict with his revealed Word in the Bible.)

CLOSING PRAYER: *Dear Abba, thank you for helping me take off and throw away the rotting rags of my old life, my old way of thinking. And thank you for clothing me in the beautiful, shining robes of a worshiper. Help me each day to choose this new wardrobe when I dress my spirit. I give you all the praise and all the glory. Amen.*

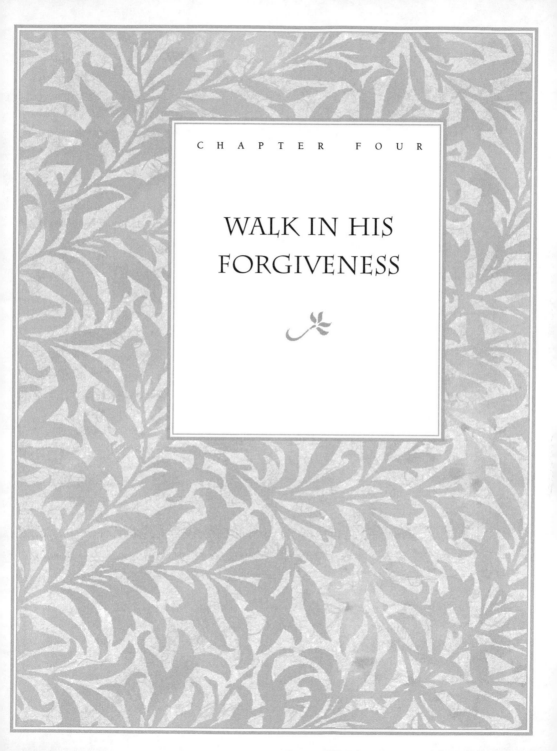

CHAPTER FOUR

WALK IN HIS
FORGIVENESS

WALK IN HIS FORGIVENESS

I remember the year our boys got an electric racetrack for Christmas. They would spend hours cheering for the little red and blue cars that raced in noisy, hypnotic loops around their room. Only one thing could shut down the action. If, at some point, the sections of track came unhooked from one another, the little cars would be derailed, and we'd have to reconnect the circuit before the race could continue.

In our spiritual race, nothing derails us faster than unforgiven sin—our own that we have not confessed and the sins of others that we have refused to forgive. Nothing breaks the circuit of God's current to and through us more surely than failing to heed this essential phrase in the essential prayer of our faith: "Forgive us our sins, just as we have forgiven those who sinned against us." (Matt. 6:12)

This prayer which Jesus taught his disciples is, in effect, the Lord's blueprint for seeking forgiveness. It contains two related requests: (1) that God would forgive our sins, and (2) that his forgiveness would come to us in proportion to the amount we have forgiven others.

MISSING THE TARGET

Before we can pray that God will forgive our sins, we must believe that we are indeed sinners, a sometimes elusive concept. It's easy to see the murderer, the child molester, the adulterer as sinners. But if we pay our taxes, don't beat our children, and live relatively respectable lives, we may feel little need for forgiveness.

Nothing could be further from the truth, no matter who we are, for the term *sin*, as used by Jesus, is an equal-opportunity concept. The New Testament uses five different words in the Greek for *sin*, the most common and comprehensive of which is *hamartia*, which literally means "missing the target."[1] So sin is, quite simply, "missing the target" with our lives. It is failing to become what we were meant to be or all that we could have been.

Who cannot relate to sin in this sense? Who can say that he or she has been as good a son or daughter, sibling or parent as possible 100 percent of the time? Who can say they have always used their gifts and talents as well as they could? Their time and energy? Who has stood up for their beliefs and convictions as faithfully as possible in every situation? Whose life measures up totally to what God had in mind? No one that I know. That is why, if we are honest with ourselves, every one of us can agree with Paul's words in Romans 3:23: "For all have sinned and fall short of the glory of God" (NIV). All of us need the forgiveness that Jesus came and died to bring us.

HOPEFUL NUDGES VS. CONDEMNING ATTACKS

I can always tell when God is convicting me of sin and leading me to confess. There is an inner nudge, a kind of restlessness that lets me know I'd better find time to spend alone with him. In that quiet time in his presence, I ask him to shine his light of holiness into all the corners of my heart and reveal to me the areas where sin is hiding. Have I hurt someone? Have I been prideful or dishonest or ungrateful?

Even though God's inner nudges are not pleasant, I am thankful for them because they prompt me to get right with him. And when they come from his heart to mine, they come with hope and a reminder that forgiveness is always available through the blood of Jesus. They encourage me to take advantage of his mercy.

But other times I am "attacked" by guilt feelings that are anything but encouraging. They accuse me as worthless, they condemn me as hopeless, and they tell me my situation is unredeemable. (When my niece, Jeanne, recognizes those condemning, hopeless feelings creeping up on her, she is inclined to say to herself, *Uh-oh! Pack your bags, you're going on a guilt trip!*) It is important for us to "distinguish between the Spirit's conviction and the Devil's nagging."[2] It is essential for us to recognize who sends us on a guilt trip. It isn't God. It is his enemy, Satan, who is called in Revelation 12:10 "the accuser." Satan makes our reservations for the trip and will even help us pack our bags, because he knows that if he can get us sidetracked in guilty feelings or keep us under a cloud of condemnation, he can deter us from God's freeing forgiveness.

CALVARY IS ENOUGH

I clearly remember a long-ago incident that managed to severely sidetrack me. In those days we had a beautiful, beloved old Irish setter named Sally who had been with us for years. One day I took Sally and my little son, Curt, with me to run a few errands. While Curt and I went into a store, we left Sally in the car momentarily with the window cracked so that she could get some air. But we must have stayed longer than I intended, because when we returned, we found her dead—suffocated. I can't describe the heartbreak of seeing my precious pet dead on the floor of the car. It was awful. And little Curt was naturally traumatized, too—as much by seeing the state I was in as by seeing the dog.

Immediately the inner accusations began. *You should never have taken Sally with you. You should have realized she needed more air. You are selfish and thoughtless. What makes you think you can raise your sons if you can't even take care of your pet?* On and on they went. Spike tried to give me some grace, but I couldn't receive it.

I walked around crying, off and on, for weeks. My emotional attitude was affecting everything about my life. My grief was becoming depression. (If you've never owned a dog, this may sound a little melodramatic to you, but if you are a pet lover, you understand. A beloved pet is truly a member of the family.)

Finally one day I got down on my knees and said, "Lord, help me. You've just got to help me."

And I heard him reason with me in the quiet room of my spirit. "Claire, these ongoing accusations are not from me. Confess your wrong and I will forgive you. I died on a cross for all sin. Do you think that what I did on the cross is sufficient payment for the wrongs of the whole world but not sufficient for the death of your dog? Are you so much worse than everyone else that you need me to do something more? No. Trust me. Calvary is enough. Come to me now. Let me forgive you and love you back to life."

I saw it so clearly then. The work of Calvary is enough. It is enough for every kind of wrong or sin—for the huge evil schemes and the small damaging acts of selfishness. (And it is enough for whatever painful or hidden sin you are struggling with right now!)

That day I confessed my selfishness and thoughtlessness as sin. I asked God to forgive me for my part in Sally's death. Very freely and very completely, he did.

COMING IN THROUGH THE RIGHT DOOR

God never sends us on a guilt trip. He makes that clear in Romans 8:1 when he says, "So now, those who are in Christ Jesus are not judged guilty." When our Father points out a wrong in our lives it always comes as an impetus toward confession (admitting wrong), repentance (turning from wrong), and receiving his forgiveness (appropriating the free gift of pardon he is holding out).

Nancy, a winsome, dark-haired, young woman I prayed with at a retreat in Illinois recently, needed God's forgiveness desperately, but she was unable to accept it as a free gift.

"I never miss church," she whispered as tears welled up in her eyes. "Even though I'm a single parent, I'm up early on Sundays to make sure my children are ready on time so we can all worship together. I attend a women's Bible study on Thursday nights, and I help with the children's choir. I kneel by my bed every single night and pray. But somehow I don't think God hears me. I still can't believe he has forgiven me for my divorce, although I've asked him to again and again. My parents warned me that my divorce would separate me from God, and they were right. I'm doing everything I know, but I can't seem to find my way back to him."

Silently I prayed, *Father, why does Nancy feel so far from you?*

And then I saw it. Nancy was trying to gain admittance to her Abba's heart through the wrong doors—doors marked "Church Attendance," "Bible Study," and "Children's Choir"—when the only way in is through the door marked "The Blood of the Lamb."

First John 1:9 provides the only road map home from a guilt trip like the one Nancy had been on. It says, "If we confess our sins, he will forgive our sins, because we can trust God to do what is right. He will cleanse us from all the wrongs we have done." Turning over new leaves, making New Year's resolutions, trying harder to be better people will never do the trick. Only the shed blood of Jesus forgives our sins and brings us back into God's presence (see Heb. 9:22; 10:17–20).

Nancy had been raised in a harsh, legalistic family, and it was very difficult to convince her that there were no deeds good enough to move her closer to God—that there was no human elbow grease powerful enough to polish her up for his approval, that she could only *receive* his gracious gift of forgiveness.

Finally Nancy was ready now to "do some business" with God. Together we bowed our heads, and she asked him to forgive her for her part in the failure of her marriage. She asked him to forgive her for trying to earn his love instead of receiving his grace. And this time when he held out his free gift of forgiveness, I believe Nancy took it. As she lifted her head, her cheeks were wet with tears. But they were tears of gratitude, not of hopelessness.

HIDDEN POCKETS OF PAIN

It is so important for us to receive God's forgiveness as Nancy did, for until we do we cannot forgive ourselves, and our entire self-concept will be diseased, distorted.

As Leanne Payne put it,

> I can be a Christian filled with the Spirit of God, but if I hate myself, the light of God is going to emanate through me in distorted ways. I will still be seeing myself through the eyes of others around me, those who perhaps could not love or affirm me . . . I will not be listening for the affirming as well as the corrective words [God] is always speaking to me, His beloved child. I will be dependent upon others . . . seeking their affirmation, their validation, and even their permission for my every move.[3]

If you, like Nancy, have within you hidden pockets of pain or guilt where you have not allowed the reality of the Lord's forgiveness to bring its healing, you may wish to "do a little business" with him yourself that will decisively settle within you the matter of your standing as his forgiven child. Here are five simple, suggested steps.

1. Begin by asking the Lord to shine his light into your heart, revealing anything that needs confessing.

2. Confess whatever sin or sin attitudes he shows you.

3. Choose to repent of these things (turn away from them— give them up).

4. Accept the Lord's forgiveness.

5. Record and date this transaction in your journal to seal what was done, then move forward from that point as "forgiven."

If you feel a need to reinforce your understanding and acceptance of God's forgiveness, you may choose to look up and write out some New Testament verses on forgiveness, perhaps one each day. Here are some suggestions: 1 John 1:9; Acts 3:19; Isaiah 55:7; Acts 13:38; Ephesians 1:7; Hebrews 9:14; Romans 8:1, 34; and Romans 10:10.

As you write each verse, claim it for yourself by rewording it in the first person, past tense. For instance, 1 John 1:9 might be reworded, "I have confessed my sin, and God has forgiven me and cleansed me from all the wrong I have done."

Read these verses aloud to yourself each morning as often as you need them; post one or two on your bathroom mirror or the dashboard of your car; make a tape of yourself reading these and other helpful verses aloud; memorize them. Do whatever you must to get these truths into your spirit. Believe them. Own them. Jesus died to purchase this forgiveness for you. Accept it!

WHO'S ON THE HOOK?

Just as the current of God's power can be blocked by our failure to confess and receive his forgiveness, so can it be blocked by our failure to forgive others. In fact, Jesus went so far as to hinge God's forgiveness on our own.

> Yes, if you forgive others for their sins, your Father in heaven will also forgive you for your sins. But if you don't forgive others, your Father in heaven will not forgive your sins. (Matt. 6:14–15)

Why would God draw such a hard line here? His heart's desire is for sweet, unbroken fellowship with us, his children, and unforgiveness on our part interrupts that fellowship. As Anglican clergyman David Watson stated, "Nothing can more quickly damage our relationship with God and with one another than an unforgiving spirit."[4]

This was definitely true in the case of Gretchen, an attractive woman in her early fifties who stayed for prayer after one of my teaching sessions at a Florida retreat. Gretchen was well aware of her bitterness toward her ex-husband but was unwilling to let it go. As a result, she had become hardened toward God. Her prayer life had all but dried up, and her husband's offenses had become an obsession.

After describing to me the verbally abusive marriage that had ended eight years earlier when her husband had left her for a younger woman, Gretchen said, "And don't tell me I need to forgive him. That would be a farce. I don't feel forgiving toward him. I don't feel anything but rage. Besides, forgiving Nick would be like saying everything he did to me and the children was okay. It would be like letting him off the hook, and I refuse to do that."

"Where is Nick now?" I asked her.

"Oh," she replied bitterly, "he's remarried and living out West. He has long since gotten over me."

"Then who is on the hook," I asked her, "Nick or you?" Her eyes registered surprise.

"I guess I am," she said.

But even though Gretchen could admit she was damaging her own life by her stubborn unforgiveness, she remained unwilling to forgive her husband. And though she allowed me to pray for her, I could feel that her spirit was tightly closed against anything the Holy Spirit might be trying to do.

When we hold others in unforgiveness, as Gretchen was doing, we are hurting ourselves by remaining in a place of death, unable to move forward with our lives. As the old saying goes, we are "renting our enemy space in our heads," for we are never truly rid of the person we have not forgiven. And worst of all, we are pitching our tents outside of a right relationship with the Father.

What I Wish I Could Have Said

There is so much I wish I could have said to Gretchen that beautiful, blue-skied day in Florida, if she had only been open enough to hear. I wish I could have told her that you don't have to *feel* forgiving to forgive. Forgiveness is not a warm, lovey-dovey feeling that comes wafting over us one day like an ocean breeze. It is a strong, deliberate, faith-based *choice*. We choose to *agree with God's word,* which tells us unforgiveness is a sin. Then we choose to act *in accordance with that word* by extending forgiveness in spite of our feelings.

I wish I could have told Gretchen that when we choose to forgive, we are not letting the other person off the hook. We are simply recognizing the difference between forgiving the person (which God has commanded us to do) and forgiving the sin (which only God can do). Our job is to forgive the person and let God deal with his or her sin. Someday we'll understand all that seems unjust to us, but for now, we can trust God's wisdom and justice (see 1 Cor. 13:12).

I wish I could have told Gretchen that only by forgiving Nick could she let her own heart out of prison and begin her own healing. And I wish I could have told her that when we feel absolutely powerless to forgive, God will send his own forgiveness through us.

I still pray for Gretchen. I pray that if the Lord gives her another chance to forgive Nick, she will be wise enough and broken enough and desperate enough to make that difficult but healing choice. Because I know her happiness depends on it.

RELEASING THE FLOW

I am realizing more and more how many negatives in our lives can be traced to unforgiveness. It affects everything! One interesting side effect of unforgiveness I've observed is its ability to block the flow of creativity within us. All of us made in God's image were designed to function as creative beings. Our creativity itself is one of the strongest ways in which we bear a family likeness to the Father. Regardless of the creative medium in which we function (whether it be poetry, pottery, or baking pies), when we are in right relation with God and our fellow human beings, his creativity will flow through us freely and joyously. But when we are holding onto bitterness or unforgiveness, our creativity is hindered and sometimes even halted altogether.

A music minister that I know well (I'll call him Brian) told me this story the other day: He had been struggling for some time with a puzzling "creative block." He found himself able to sing well everywhere but in his own church. When he did youth concerts or performed in other churches, he was pleased with his performance, but when he was scheduled to sing a solo in his own church, he could almost feel his throat beginning to close up, and his singing fell far below par.

Then one day while praying with a group of friends, one of them sensed that there was someone Brian needed to forgive. Brian examined his heart but could think of no one against whom he was holding a grudge. Still his friend persisted.

"It's like I see a water pipe that is clogged," his friend said. "And the water won't flow again until you forgive whoever it is."

The group prayed again, and as they were praying, Brian remembered an incident in which his senior pastor had jokingly made a belittling remark about him in front of some choir members. That had been more than six months earlier, but Brian realized he had been harboring an underground resentment toward his senior pastor ever since.

Brian chose right then to forgive his pastor and thought little more about it until he stood up the next Sunday to sing a solo in his own church. His beautiful tenor voice soared forth unhindered with such freedom and power that everyone was surprised, but no one more so than Brian himself! God revealed to Brian that his gift had been held hostage by his unforgiveness.

When my friend Judith, a songwriter, chose to forgive the publishing company that had treated her badly in a contractual agreement, a flood of new songs began to spring forth from her almost effortlessly. And this came after almost a year of what she had called "a serious dry spell."

Few creative Christians would argue with the fact that our gifts originate with God and flow through us. The great composer, Giacomo Puccini, said of perhaps his greatest masterpiece, *Madame Butterfly*, "The music of this opera was dictated to me by God; I was merely instrumental in putting it on paper and communicating it to the public."[5] If God is the Water Tower, our gifts are the water, and we are the pipes, we had best take care to keep those pipes clean of unforgiveness, or we may miss a masterpiece that's trying to come through!

Jesus advises us in Matthew 5:23–24 to make peace with our brothers and sisters before leaving our gifts at the altar. As we learn to heed this advice, we will find, as both Brian and Judith did, that our gifts are purified and maximized and made presentable by our willingness to forgive and be forgiven.

LOVING HANDS ON OUR SHOULDERS

Forgiving others need not be a face-to-face confrontation. God's power can transcend huge obstacles, working in lives that are separated by miles and even years. I was blessed to see at close range the healing that came into the heart of a young woman named Grace when she forgave her father years after his death.

Grace is a single mother who was involved in a Christian Twelve-Step group with me a number of years ago. Her childhood had not been a happy one. Her alcoholic father had been a brilliant but brutal man whose inconsistent behavior had kept Grace in constant turmoil.

In our Twelve-Step group, we had been given an assignment for the week by Ann, our group facilitator, to invite Jesus and his healing love back into one wounding childhood memory.

"But those things happened so long ago," Grace protested uneasily. "Wouldn't we be better off just forgetting the past and moving forward?"

"No," Ann explained. "There is no going forward until we forgive. Unforgiveness is a poison that affects every part of our lives. It may feel difficult or even impossible, but Jesus can give us his power to forgive. He can go back with us into those past situations and bring healing into long-buried wounds."

The next week when Ann asked for a volunteer to share the results of the forgiveness assignment, Grace's was the first hand to go up.

"The scene I picked was the living room where I used to do my homework," Grace explained. "It was a terrible time, waiting for my dad to get home from work. I was usually so nervous. But as I closed my eyes in prayer, I could see Jesus there in the room with me. He was standing right behind the big, flowered chair where I used to sit, and he had his hands on my shoulders.

"Then all of a sudden I heard the scratch of Dad's key in the lock. That sound always made me panic because I'd think, *Will he be sober or drunk?* Remembering it all, I suddenly felt a tremendous rage toward this man who wrecked my childhood.

"Then Dad walked into my memory, and I saw him just as clearly as I'm seeing you sitting in this room. I remembered the suit he had on and the briefcase he was carrying, and I remembered that expression in his eyes. He was drunk. Really drunk.

"For a long time I stared at that memory of my dad, still feeling the hands of Jesus on my shoulders. And it was like God's love and forgiveness for my dad came right through those hands and into me. And when I spoke out loud, I thought it would be the voice of a child, but it was my voice.

"I said to that memory, 'Oh, Daddy, I forgive you. And I love you. I do.'"

In essence the whole Bible is a story of forgiveness. It is the story of a Creator-God who loved his creation so much that he chose to forgive. He chose to send his Son to love us and die for us so that we who are made in his image can live as he lives—magnanimously, charitably, graciously—toward others. And because of his love, it is possible. Because of the love of the Crucified One standing behind us, because of his nail-pierced hands resting on our shoulders, filling us with his power, we are able to live and love as God's forgiven and forgiving children.

WALK IN HIS FORGIVENESS: 1

DON'T WAIT TO PRAY

*Read and reflect on these verses of Scripture
and the letter from your Abba that follows.*

God, you know what I have done wrong;
 I cannot hide my guilt from you. Ps. 69:5

Let us, then, feel very sure that we can come before God's throne where there is grace. There we can receive mercy and grace to help us when we need it. Heb. 4:16

In Christ we can come before God with freedom and without fear. We can do this through faith in Christ. Eph. 3:12

My Child,

Don't try to hide your failure from me. Don't try to resolve your conflicts on your own before you come to me. That is like trying to clean up your house for the housekeeper! Instead, run into my presence with the confidence of a beloved child, for that is who you are to me. Bring me your sins and failures. Lay them on my altar and confess them. Don't you know that I see you as you are and yet I love you? Because of what my Son, Jesus, has done for you there is mercy waiting. Because of him, whatever you confess I will forgive, and whatever you have failed in I will redeem. Don't wait until you are better. This life of prayer is a "come-as-you-are" affair.

So, come!
Abba

WRITE A LETTER TO YOUR ABBA: 1

PRAYERS OF REPENTANCE
AND FORGIVENESS

*After reading and reflecting on God's words to you, write your own letter
to him in your journal or in the space below, using the following guide:*

1. See Jesus taking you by the hand and leading you through large, heavy
   doors, into the Father's house. Hear him telling you that you may run
   to his Father and tell him anything. Hear him encourage you to confess
   your sin and receive God's forgiveness. Now, go to your Father in
   prayer. Climb up into his lap. What do you say to him in prayer. What
   do you confess? What is his reply? Write out all these things in your letter to Abba God.

   Dear Abba,

   _____

   _____

   _____

2. Now put down your pen. Ask Abba to speak to you. Sit quietly for ten
   minutes (or more) and listen to him in your heart. What is he saying to
   you about your freedom to confess? What personal words of love, guidance, or challenge do you hear? Write these out in your journal.
   (Remember, God's word in your heart will never conflict with his
   revealed Word in the Bible.)

   CLOSING PRAYER: *Dear Abba, I am so humbled by your love—by
   realizing that you know everything about me and yet you love me anyway. Thank you for the freedom to confess and the gift of forgiveness. Let
   me never take it for granted. I love you, Lord. Amen.*

WALK IN HIS FORGIVENESS: 2

IN REPENTANCE YOU WILL
FIND REST AND PEACE

For thus saith the Lord GOD, the Holy One of Israel; In returning and rest shall ye be saved; in quietness and in confidence shall be your strength. ISA. 30:15 KJV

So you must change your hearts and lives! Come back to God, and he will forgive your sins. Then the Lord will send the time of rest. ACTS 3:19

Dearest Child,

Once I have forgiven your sin, I want you to repent. What is repentance? It is more than a feeling of remorse over what you have done. It is the act of turning away from what you have done and choosing not to do it again. Repentance is returning to me. This is what I am calling you to do, my child. Turn away from your sin and toward my mercy. For in repentance, in returning, you will find rest and peace. In my presence you will find your confidence, and in my love you will find your strength. So turn around, my child, and come home to me today. My arms are open.

Forever your,
Abba

WRITE A LETTER TO YOUR ABBA: 2
PRAYERS OF REPENTANCE
AND FORGIVENESS

1. See yourself driving on a long interstate highway. You feel certain you are going in the wrong direction, and you feel terrible about that. But feeling terrible does not turn your car around. You make a decision to turn back. You exit at the next exit ramp and head back in the other direction. As you do, the day begins to grow light around you. In your journal or in the space below, tell the Father how this scene relates to your understanding of repentance. Tell him about specific "turning" times you can remember on your Christian journey. Is the Lord telling you to turn around now?

Dear Abba,

2. Now put down your pen. Ask Abba to speak to you. Sit quietly for ten minutes (or more) and listen to him in your heart. What is he saying to you about repentance? What personal words of love, guidance, or challenge do you hear? Write these out in your journal. (Remember, God's word in your heart will never conflict with his revealed Word in the Bible.)

CLOSING PRAYER: *Dear Abba, I long to be right with you. There is no peace in my life when I'm going in the wrong direction. There is no joy on my journey when I'm not traveling with your Holy Spirit. Show me where I am going wrong, and give me the courage to turn around. In Jesus' name, Amen.*

WALK IN HIS FORGIVENESS: 3
STEP INTO MY LIGHT

Here is the message we have heard from Christ and now announce to you: God is light, and in him there is no darkness at all. 1 JOHN 1:5

Your word is like a lamp for my feet
and a light for my path. PS. 119:105

If we confess our sins, he is faithful and just to forgive us our sins, and to cleanse us from all unrighteousness. 1 JOHN 1:9 KJV

My Child,

Be sure of this: I will not reveal any sin in you that I cannot forgive. Stay close to me. Continue to read my Word and pray. My Word works in partnership with your prayer. It shines a searchlight into the shadows of your soul, revealing the subtle, sinful attitudes that hide there: the fear, the arrogance, the dishonesty, the bitterness. And once you've seen those wrong attitudes, your prayer can lasso them with ropes of conviction and present them to me to be forgiven. Step into my light and know the joy of my forgiveness.

Come to me now,
Abba

WRITE A LETTER TO YOUR ABBA: 3
PRAYERS OF REPENTANCE
AND FORGIVENESS

1. In your letter to Abba God, invite him to shine the light of his Spirit into the corners of your life, revealing to you where you need to confess, repent, forgive others or yourself. (This is an ongoing exercise, so return to it often.) In your journal or in the space below, write out your confessions. Receive God's forgiveness. Be prepared to confess to or forgive others.

Dear Abba,

_____

_____

_____

_____

_____

2. Now put down your pen. Ask Abba to speak to you. Sit quietly for ten minutes (or more) and listen to him in your heart. What is he saying to you about his Word as the light? What personal words of love, guidance, or challenge do you hear? Write these out in your journal. (Remember, God's word in your heart will never conflict with his revealed Word in the Bible.)

CLOSING PRAYER: *Dear Abba, I am so prone to hide my defects from everyone else and from myself that I sometimes forget you see everything. I don't want to hide anymore. I want to be clean and right in your sight. Thank you for your Word that shines a searchlight into my soul and reveals my need for confession, repentance, and forgiveness. Help me cooperate with you, no matter what you show me. In Jesus' name, Amen.*

WALK IN HIS FORGIVENESS: 4
I WILL HELP YOU WEED
YOUR GARDEN

Do not judge, and you will not be judged. Do not condemn, and you will not be condemned. Forgive, and you will be forgiven. LUKE 6:37 NIV

Dear Child,

Your life is like a garden. But what is growing there? Is it the beautiful flowers of peace and righteousness and love? Or is your garden choked with the weeds of judgment and condemnation and unforgiveness? If these weeds are left unpulled they will suffocate your life. They will cause you to nurse every injustice and rehearse every wrong, real or imagined. They will keep you rooted in the soil of death, poisoning everything around you, for nothing good can grow in the same garden with these deadly weeds. So, before they grow any bigger let me help you pull them from your heart. The weeds of judgment and condemnation can only be "pulled up" by confessing them as sin and receiving my forgiveness. Is there an instance in which you have judged and condemned? Is there someone you have not forgiven? Remember, as you judge others, so will I judge you. So confess your unforgiveness and allow my mercy to grow in you.

Let me help you weed your garden,
Abba

WRITE A LETTER TO YOUR ABBA: 4

PRAYERS OF REPENTANCE
AND FORGIVENESS

1. See yourself in the garden of your heart with Jesus. In your garden are beautiful flowers, but growing in among them are weeds of judgment and condemnation. Jesus wants to help you pull them. But first he wants to help you see why they are springing up and against whom. In your letter to Abba, describe the weeds that are spoiling your garden. Whom have you been judgmental toward? Confess this and let Jesus help you pull the weeds.

Dear Abba,

_____

_____

_____

2. Now put down your pen. Ask Abba to speak to you. Sit quietly for ten minutes (or more) and listen to him in your heart. What is he saying to you about judging others? What personal words of love, guidance, or challenge do you hear? Write these out in your journal. (Remember, God's word in your heart will never conflict with his revealed Word in the Bible.)

CLOSING PRAYER: *Dear Abba, forgive my readiness to look into other lives and make snap judgments about things I don't understand. Forgive my prejudices. And forgive me for judging my enemies, those who have hurt me. I place them in your hands and leave the judging to you, knowing that you know and understand all things and that your justice is perfect. Amen.*

WALK IN HIS FORGIVENESS: 5

FORGIVE FREELY

The kingdom of heaven is like a king who decided to collect the money his servants owed him. . . . A servant who owed him several million dollars was brought to him. But the servant did not have enough money to pay. . . . [So he] fell on his knees and begged, "Be patient with me, and I will pay you everything I owe." The master felt sorry for the servant and told him he did not have to pay it back. . . . Later, that same servant found another servant who owed him a few dollars. The servant grabbed him around the neck and said, "Pay me the money you owe me!" The other servant fell on his knees and begged him, "Be patient with me, and I will pay you everything I owe." But the first servant refused to be patient. He threw the other servant into prison until he could pay everything he owed. . . . Then the master called his servant in and said, "You evil servant! . . . You should have showed mercy to that other servant, just as I showed mercy to you."
MATT. 18:23–33

My Child,

I am calling you to forgive as I forgive—to look into the life of your husband, your wife, your neighbor, your friend, even your enemy and extend mercy as I have extended it to you. How can you, having been forgiven everything, hold anything against another? My forgiveness comes to you as a gift. The price for that gift has been paid by my Son, who died so that you can walk in freedom. In the joy of that reality, you should be moving through the world extending mercy to everyone—proclaiming peace and love and the end of all hostility. Come know the elation of living like this—of taking no hostages, of holding no prisoners, of setting captives free with the key of forgiveness!

Forgive freely, my child,
Abba

WRITE A LETTER TO YOUR ABBA: 5
PRAYERS OF REPENTANCE
AND FORGIVENESS

1. See yourself ragged and hungry and locked in a prison cell on a long hallway of other cells, each one housing another ragged prisoner. Jesus is walking down the hallway. He stops at your cell and takes a large, brass key from the pocket of his robe. He unlocks your cell door. He gives you food and clean clothes; then, placing the key in your hands, he instructs you to unlock the other prisoners and set them free. Write about this in your letter. Tell Abba how you will respond to his Son's instructions.

Dear Abba,

---

2. Now put down your pen. Ask Abba to speak to you. Sit quietly for ten minutes (or more) and listen to him in your heart. What is he saying to you about forgiving others? What personal words of love, guidance, or challenge do you hear? Write these out in your journal. (Remember, God's word in your heart will never conflict with his revealed Word in the Bible.)

CLOSING PRAYER: *Dear Abba, so many times I have kept other people in a prison of unforgiveness, forgetting that you have unlocked my prison cell and set me free. Forgive me and help me to use my faith to set others free. I want to live and love as Jesus did. Make me more like him. Amen.*

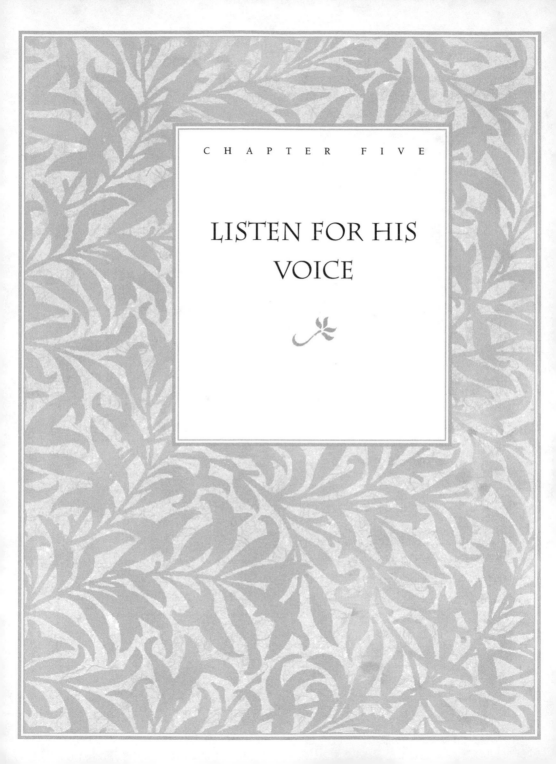

LISTEN FOR HIS VOICE

LISTEN FOR HIS VOICE

I'll never forget the early morning at McDonald's that I ran into Greg, an old friend from my amateur theater days. Greg is a kind of latter-day hippie type who usually dresses like he's playing a role in some historical drama. He's also a very gifted artist.

"How's it goin', Greg?" I asked casually, not expecting a detailed answer.

"Do you really want to know?" Greg asked, and I felt compelled to answer, "Yes."

Well, it was one of those long stories. After months of depression Greg had been in counseling, dealing with what he called "childhood issues."

"My parents never beat me or anything like that," he explained. "My old man just had this way of making me feel worthless. He'd say things to me like, 'You know, son, you'll never amount to anything if you keep this up,' or 'I knew it was just a matter of time before you'd screw things up. You always do.'

"Those old negative messages were always playing in my head, so

121

even when things would start going great in my life, I'd find a way to screw them up."

A MENTAL THEME SONG

"You know, I even had my own theme song playing in there," Greg continued, tapping his index finger to his temple.

"Your own theme song?" Being a songwriter, I was fascinated.

"Yeah. You know that old country tune 'Born to Lose'? Well, sometimes I'd find myself humming it saying to myself, 'Yep, that's me—born to lose.'"

"So what has your therapy been like?" I wanted to know.

"Well," he replied, "my therapist has been using a thing called 'replacement therapy.' She's got me monitoring my thoughts, and every time I hear one of those negative, downer messages from my childhood, I stop it in its tracks and replace it with some other words."

"What other words?" I asked.

"Oh, it can be anything," Greg explained. "Even something as simple as saying the ABCs, as long as it stops the negative tape."

"The ABCs? What possible good can they do? Listen, Greg," I said effusively, "have I got some words for you!"

Well, Greg knows that I'm a Christian, and being Jewish himself, I'm afraid he thought he was in for an evangelical sales job. I could feel him beginning to inch away from me.

"Hey, wait a minute," I said. "You don't even have to get into our side of the book to get to the good stuff. You guys have some great words on your side, too. Like, for instance, 'The Lord is my Shepherd, I shall not want.' That beats the ABCs all to pieces."

THE POWER OF THE WORDS WE LISTEN TO

I have no idea whether Greg ever abandoned his ABC replacement therapy for the power of the Old Testament psalms. But that conversation really got me thinking about the words we unconsciously listen to in our minds and hearts. They truly have the power to shape our lives.

If this were the kind of world that God intended it to be, there would be no stories like Greg's. All parents would be speaking love and truth to their children from the time they were born. Unfortunately, the world has veered off course. Some of us grew up in homes where the words we heard were as deadly as poison. And even those of us who heard positive messages from our parents took in negative ones from our culture, our peers, our teachers, our coaches—in short, from the world around us.

In his book *Reflections*, Paul Tournier put forth the idea that much of our behavior can be traced to the words and perceptions to which our minds repeatedly return. These words in our minds do not just affect us once. They are like recordings we take out to replay again and again throughout our lives.

I can think of words in my childhood that affected me. Some were simple remarks, probably spoken without a great deal of thought, yet they have stayed in my mind.

For example, I recall a remark made when I was ten as clearly as

if it were made yesterday. That year I had a huge crush on an ener-
getic, wise-cracking classmate named Tommy. I thought every word
out of his mouth was hilarious—until one day when I was walking
home from school with my friend Lynn.

"Hey, cookie!" I heard someone yell from behind us. I knew that
voice! It was Tommy's! I wheeled around expectantly, my ten-year-
old heart squarely on my sleeve.

"Not you, cupcake!" he said in his perfect-putdown tone of voice.
Crushed? That's putting it mildly. Mind you, I wasn't even sure what
Tommy's idea of a cupcake was, but I went through most of my ado-
lescence feeling like I probably was one! That silly, thoughtless
remark was made decades ago, yet I can remember exactly where I
was when I heard it and how it made me feel.

In contrast to that negative crack, I recall with equal clarity a
compliment paid to me when I was even younger. In second grade
I idolized my student teacher, Miss Sutton, who had beautiful natural curls and a peaches-and-cream complexion. One day as she
walked around the room checking our work, Miss Sutton stopped
at my desk.

Picking up my paper and gazing at it approvingly, she said,
"Claire, you are developing a beautiful handwriting."

Wow! What a high! She handed my paper back to me, and I examined it in a new light, marveling over the loops and curves of this new
cursive writing we were learning. *Beautiful,* I thought. *Beautiful!*

After that remark, I asked Mom to get me some stationery of my
own, and I began writing letters to out-of-town relatives. That year
for my birthday, I got my first diary. I developed a love of putting

words on paper. Who knows? Perhaps the very fact that I am a writer today was influenced by that chance remark from my much-admired teacher.

SELECTING THE PROGRAM AND PROGRAMMER

Our minds and spirits are much like computers. They take in the words that are directed at us without screening them for accuracy. We must be alert to what is being programmed in, which words we choose to store in our permanent memory. Also, it is up to us to decide who we will allow to "punch the buttons" of our keyboards.

Sadly, many of us, even some of us who have entered into a relationship with the Lord, leave our keyboards wide open to anybody's program. We spend more hours in front of the television set, allowing our spirits to be programmed by the world's temporal shallowness, than we spend giving God's Word a chance to program our spirits with his truth. We spend more mental energy rehearsing those old negative messages from the past than we spend replacing them with the healing words God would speak to us today if only we would listen.

Many centuries ago Paul spoke clearly about the danger of dwelling on the wrong messages. In Romans 12:2, he warns us: "Do not conform any longer to the pattern of this world, but be transformed by the renewing of your mind" (NIV).

How are our minds renewed and transformed? There is a "spiritual replacement therapy" which allows us to discard the world's subtle lies and damaging epithets and begin replacing them with God's words of healing and redemption. Like changing the disk in a computer, we consciously bring up God's program and invite his words to mold us into the image of his Son.

LIFE-GIVING SPIRIT WORDS

Why are God's words so powerfully able to work within us? They are more than letters on paper. They are more than sounds on the airwaves. They contain the life-giving power of the Holy Spirit. Jesus said in John 6:63, "The words I told you are spirit, and they give life."

As we come to the Lord in prayer, we should be learning to listen, making ample space for God's words to come into our hearts and spirits. But many Christians I talked to as I was writing this chapter were honest enough to confess that in their prayer lives, they do most of the talking. Many candidly admitted they weren't exactly sure how to listen to God.

It is crucial that we learn to listen to the right voice in our spirits, for if we don't we will end up listening to the wrong ones. As Leanne Payne has said,

> Listening prayer is a vital facet of God's presence with us. It is a place of freedom from the voices of the world, the flesh, and the devil. Those latter voices, when hearkened to and obeyed, pull us toward nonbeing and death. To fail to listen to God is to be listening to one or another (or all) of those voices. It is to miss the vital walk in the Spirit and our immensely creative collaboration with him.[1]

Learning to listen for his word to us, deciding to let ourselves be programmed by his truth, is to place ourselves in the presence of the One who became the Word Incarnate—God's truth in a human body. And as we receive his words of life into our spirits, that's exactly what he will make of us—human containers for the truth and power of his living Word!

BELIEVING HE IS THERE

How do we cooperate in becoming containers for his truth? First, we must move beyond "believing in him" to believing that he is actually there, waiting to welcome us and desiring to communicate with us. There is a big difference.

For instance, you probably "believe in" the president of the United States. You have seen him on television and read about him in the newspapers. You do not doubt his existence. But do you believe that if you flew to Washington, D.C., and stopped by the White House, he would stop whatever he was doing to have a personal conference with you? Probably not.

This is the problem many of us have as we approach God. Like Ashleigh, a young woman several of us prayed for at a women's conference in Colorado, some Christians have a hard time believing God has time for them.

Ashleigh's father was a physician who had worked long, hard hours during her childhood. After his tedious, demanding workdays, he would come home weary and distracted. At a young age, Ashleigh would try to get his attention, try to sit on his lap or engage him in conversation. But this would invariably irritate him, and his anger would flare.

So she learned to watch him furtively from across the room, hungry for his attention but afraid of his anger. As she would watch him sit in stony silence, sipping a drink and reading the newspaper, Ashleigh understood that *"Daddy is not to be disturbed."*

In her early teens, Ashleigh committed her life to Christ. She loved her church youth group, and longed to have a prayer life. But whenever she tried to pray, she would feel self-conscious and tongue-tied. She would feel certain that her prayers must be bothering God or interrupting him or wasting his time. When she closed her eyes, she could picture him like the statue of Abraham Lincoln in the Lincoln Memorial, a huge stone man seated in a chair staring down in total, unfeeling silence.

Our prayers for Ashleigh were prayers of healing—not for her body or her mind but for her image of God as her heavenly Father. We asked him to let her know that he was indeed there, waiting to welcome her and desiring to communicate with her. We asked him to heal the inner wounds caused by her earthly father's rejection so that he could begin revealing his deep, unchanging love for her.

BEGIN WHERE YOU ARE

That fall day in Colorado, I recommended to Ashleigh something that was recommended to me years before by John Barr, a good friend and a man of faith from whom I have learned much.

"You can only begin where you are," John used to say to us. "To start out by saying that you trust God when you don't is a charade. Instead, bring as much of yourself as you know to as much of God as you understand, and begin there."

As Ashleigh came before her heavenly Father that day, her prayer was something like this:

"Father, you know me," she prayed. "You know all the things in my childhood that have kept me from you. I have tried to get over those things on my own, but I can't. I don't want to stay like this. I'm sorry I have blamed you. I want a relationship with you. Heal me and teach me to trust you. Help me forgive my dad. Help me not to confuse his rejection with your love. I want to hear from you, God. I need to know that it's okay to talk to you about anything, and I need to know that you will *answer.*"

Like Ashleigh, each one of us who desires the give and take of a real friendship with God will benefit from coming to him in a prayer of openness, bringing as much of ourselves as we know to as much of him as we understand. When we express our need for his words, our willingness to listen, and our hope to be changed, we are readying ourselves to hear his voice.

FINDING A QUIET PLACE AND TIME

Linda Schubert, in her practical little pamphlet on prayer, *Miracle Hour,* suggests that "Christians who sincerely want to progress in [their] relationship with the Lord . . . must find a quiet place, away from noisy distractions. . . . He wants to speak to us more than we want to listen. He is a God of love, and love longs to communicate."[2]

In our crazy, noisy world, this may be the most difficult part of listening prayer. But since drawing aside purposefully and expectantly is the surest way to hear God's inner word, we must search until we find that quiet time and place.

Spike and I live in a wonderfully tranquil spot in the country. Our two sons are grown and married now. Obviously, quiet time for listening to the Lord is far easier to find these days for us than it was when the children were very young, when Spike worked a demanding job, and we lived in a busy city.

When your children are active toddlers, you may find it necessary to lock the door of your room just to grab a quiet moment to catch your breath. During those busy years, your best hope for time with the Lord may be to set your alarm and get up before the rest of your family or to stay awake after they have gone to sleep.

Wherever you are in life (whether married or single, with a full or empty nest, in a tranquil or a busy setting) time alone for listening to the Lord is vital and possible, even if it is not easy. The Lord himself will help you find that time and place.

SLOWING DOWN AND FOCUSING

Even when we know God is there waiting to speak, even when we have found a time and a place to meet with him, it will be difficult for many of us to slow down and focus. We develop a rhythm of doing and accomplishing and achieving that makes sitting still feel unnatural and even uncomfortable.

Luke 10:38 portrays two very different sisters who welcomed

Jesus into their home. Martha was so caught up in her preparations for his visit that she was not even able to sit down and spend time with him. Mary, on the other hand, sat at his feet, raptly listening to his words and drinking in his presence. The fourteenth-century Christian classic *The Cloud of Unknowing* describes Mary this way: "She gazed [at him] with all the love of her heart. Nothing she saw or heard could budge her, but there she sat, completely still, with deep delight, and an urgent love eagerly reaching out. . . . From 'this part,' nothing on earth could move her."[3]

What a beautiful picture of listening with love! But Martha was not impressed. She resented her sister's tranquillity. If you've got even a touch of Martha in you, you know there is nothing that irritates a Martha in action more than to spy a Mary tranquilly "doing nothing."

But Jesus made it clear, when Martha complained to him, that Mary's "work" was by far "the better part." From his divine perspective, listening is higher than doing.

I would even take it a step further. I believe that listening should always precede doing. I would not be the least bit surprised to find that what Mary heard at the feet of Jesus later led her into some certain work or some change of focus in her life. This seems to be the flow of things. Hearing from God almost always prompts and prepares us to take action of some sort based on what we've heard. But we invariably go wrong when we rush into action before we have stopped and listened.

Mary had the ability to turn from activity, to slow down and focus on him and his words for her. She had a heart to hear, and that endeared her to the Lord.

LIKE A BABY'S CRY OR A CONTROL TOWER

God is always looking for a believer like Mary who is willing to stop, tune in, and listen for his words.

"This is the one I esteem," he said through the prophet Isaiah, "he who is humble and contrite in spirit, and trembles at my word" (Isa. 66:2 NIV).

How can we become more like Mary? In a world that values doing and achieving more than listening, how can we develop the contemplative heart that is willing to stop and hear?

In my own life, it was only as I began to understand the importance of hearing God that I began to hear him. It was then that the ears of my spirit tuned in.

This is exactly the same principle as learning to listen for the cry of a newborn. I remember bringing Curt, our first son, home from the hospital. I was in awe of my responsibility as a new mother. I had always been a sound sleeper, and I was afraid I might not hear him in the night when he cried. So before drifting off to sleep each night of those first few weeks, I would remind myself to listen. I would ask God to help me hear. And because I was convinced of the importance of hearing that little cry, I never slept through it.

The importance of listening is something every airline pilot knows. I learned this recently from a young pilot named Larry with whom I shared a cab on the way to the airport in Louisiana. Larry had only recently earned his solo license and had purchased his own plane for use in his business.

"Are you ever afraid when you're flying?" I asked him.

Larry acknowledged that during his first year as a pilot he had found "flying blind" (in weather conditions that prevent pilots from seeing what is around them) very unnerving.

"But once you get used to listening to the tower and getting your bearings and direction from their instructions," he said, "it starts to feel natural. The important thing is to know your position in relation to the tower."

Proverbs 18:10 tells us that "the LORD is like a strong tower; those who do right can run to him for safety." Like a control tower with Spirit radar, our Father broadcasts his directions to us when the circumstances of our lives have forced us to "fly blind." Tuning in to the tower is our way of safety in all kinds of weather.

SCRIPTURE, SONGS, AND SPIRIT WHISPERS

Once we have come into the quiet, once we have stilled our hearts, focused our minds, and tuned into the "control tower," God's word comes to us in a number of ways.

1. The Bible

Anglican priest David Watson referred to the Bible as "our final court of appeal as to what God has said. Here is the God-given objective test for our belief and behavior."[4] The Bible is always the obvious place to begin when listening for the Lord in times of personal worship.

So many times I have sought God's wisdom on something, praying, "Lord, show me your will on such-and-such," when all the while his answer was clearly laid out in Scripture. I had just never taken the time to seek out what was already written there.

I remember plainly a time when Spike and I were struggling with a financial issue and truly wanted God's guidance as to what we should do, but we couldn't seem to hear from him. Much later when we enrolled in Crown Ministries, a small-group financial study,[5] we found that the answer to our financial question had been in the Bible all along. In fact, we discovered that there are forty-three hundred Scripture verses related to finance in the Bible! We learned through that experience to look first to his Word for guidance!

Jesus himself lived by Scripture. He knew it, taught from it, and saw himself as the fulfillment of its every prophetic utterance. Bible scholar J. I. Packer has called the Bible "Christ's textbook."[6] If Jesus, who was God's own Son, turned to Scripture for his Father's words, surely we can do the same with confidence. Scripture is the starting line for those who wish to run the race according to the Father's will.

2. The Work of Christian Writers and Composers

Though our basic source of truth is the Bible, my personal worship time is enriched by the writings and compositions of other Christians.

Almost every day of my Christian journey I have read *My Utmost for His Highest,* the daily devotional writing of Oswald Chambers, a Scottish teacher and preacher whose spiritual vision penetrates God's heart unlike any other writer I have ever read. Although reading Chambers is frequently uncomfortable for me because his challenges and exhortations hit me squarely between the eyes, I always close his book with some message from God that is personal and powerful.

C. S. Lewis explains spiritual realities for me with unparalleled clarity. Max Lucado's prose sings like poetry. Brennan Manning makes God's grace personal and real. Joni Eareckson Tada brings the gift of vulnerability to her books, making me feel that I've just had a visit with a close friend. Richard Foster's books are so rich with biblical reality that I have to take them in small bites, concentrating on a few paragraphs at a time, but when I finish one, I am thoroughly nourished. Leanne Payne has been my tour guide on a journey toward inner healing and a deeper prayer life.

Another way I hear from God is through the melodies and lyrics of good music. During my quiet time, I enjoy reading (or listening to) the lyrics of Christian writers ranging from Twila Paris to Fanny Crosby, from Martin Luther to Wayne Watson. I also find that listening to inspirational instrumental music stirs up God's silent words in my spirit.

The gifted writers listed above (and many others) help me hear from God. They let me see his truth from many perspectives like a diamond with many facets. Through their words God speaks to me, showing me who he is and what he is able to do in a surrendered life.

3. Whispers of His Holy Spirit

The most personal way of hearing from God is by learning to listen for the still, small voice of his Holy Spirit. The Holy Spirit acts as an interpreter who unlocks spiritual mysteries. He points to Jesus and causes us to recall his words. He provides the discernment we need to tell the pure truth of God from the enemy's subtle shading of reality. He is a guide, leading us in the right direction. He is a comforter, easing our pain in times of grief. He is the One who dwells in us as the closest of friends, bringing with him the power of our risen Lord.

Paul's prayer in Ephesians is that we can know the fullness of this power in our lives.

> I pray also that you . . . will know that God's power is very great for us who believe. That power is *the same as the great strength God used to raise Christ from the dead* and put him at his right side in the heavenly world. (Eph. 1:18–20, emphasis mine)

This promised power—the same supernatural energy that raised Jesus from the dead—is an amazing and dynamic force! There is no way we can manufacture power like that on our own. We can't drum it up by believing hard enough or trying with all our might to be good Christians. We can only receive it when we open ourselves to God's Spirit.

On the day of Pentecost, the disciples stayed in prayer until the Holy Spirit came upon them. A rushing wind and tongues of fire accompanied his coming, and the disciples began speaking in other languages through his power (see Acts 2).

I know some people who have had earth-moving experiences with the Holy Spirit not unlike the day of Pentecost, and I know others whose experience has been less dramatic but every bit as real. Either way, we can be certain that when we ask our good Father for his indwelling Spirit, he never, never turns us away. We have his Word on that!

> If your children ask for a fish, which of you would give them a snake instead? Or, if your children ask for an egg, would you give them a scorpion? Even though you are bad, you know how to give good things to your children. *How much more your heavenly Father will give the Holy Spirit to those who ask him!* (Luke 11:11–13, *emphasis mine*)

If we belong to Jesus, his Father and his Spirit have been here with us since we gave him our lives. They are an inseparable Trinity. But there is a deeper dimension of Holy Spirit reality that is available to us when we invite the Spirit's full involvement in our lives—a dimension that empowers our ministries, enriches our prayer lives, and adds excitement to our spiritual journeys.

I've often heard that the Holy Spirit is a gentleman who will never force his way into the power position in our lives. But when we invite him to come in, he readily accepts our invitation.

Have you ever issued an invitation like this to the Holy Spirit? Have you ever given him permission to enter every part of your life, bringing his power? If not, you may be longing to do that right now. There is no formula, no set ritual, no fixed prayer to pray. If your heart is surrendered to the Lord, you can pray a prayer like this one in total confidence:

Come, Holy Spirit, and dwell in me. Fill my surrendered heart with the love of Jesus. Let it flow through me as the sap of the vine flows through its branches. Convict me of my sins. Wash me with his cleansing blood. Flood me with his mercy. Fill me with all the power, the wisdom, and the faith I will need to bring Jesus to a wounded world. Heal me, Holy Spirit, so that I can bring healing. Comfort me so that I can bring comfort. Guide me in the way I should walk, and empower me to follow. Whisper to me in your still, small voice, and teach my heart to listen. Come, Holy Spirit, come. I wait on you.

I would suggest a time of listening silence after praying such a prayer. Write down whatever the Lord is speaking to you. If he convicts you of some unconfessed area of sin, confess it immediately and let him take it. Then receive all that he has for you—all of his mercy, power, and healing. Finally, let him fill you with his words of worship as you praise him for the gift of himself.

Because I am a "leaky vessel," I need to pray a prayer like the one above frequently, asking the Holy Spirit for refilling and refueling. Then I listen for the intimate whispers of his voice in my spirit. They speak of the love of my Abba, my friend, and remind me of my Savior's nearness. Those whispers always draw me into a deeper life of prayer.

THE CHAIR BY THE BEDSIDE

Brennan Manning tells the story of an old man who longed for a deeper life of prayer. After trying unsuccessfully to comprehend scholarly books on the subject, he finally tried praying in a very childlike manner—by picturing Jesus seated in the chair beside his bed and talking to him. He found that he liked it so much, he did it "a couple of hours every day."

When the old man fell ill, he confessed to the local priest this habit of daily "having a conversation with Jesus."

"I'm careful, though," he told the priest. "If my daughter saw me talking to an empty chair she'd . . . send me off to the funny farm." The priest, profoundly moved by the old man's story, promised not to reveal his secret.

Two days later the old man's daughter called the priest to tell him of her father's death.

"Did he seem to die in peace?" the priest asked. The daughter assured him that her father had indeed gone quite peacefully.

"But there was something strange, Father," she said reflectively. "In fact beyond strange, kinda weird. Apparently just before Daddy died, he leaned over and rested his head on a chair beside the bed."[7]

This old man knew his Abba. He had learned to share the kind of intimate friendship with his heavenly Father that is available to each of us today. Our Abba is waiting for us to slow down, to come to him and sit by his chair (as this old man did, as Mary did) and listen to his voice. He is the friend who is always there—the one who does the "magnificent work of converting the 'desert of loneliness' within into the spaciously beautiful 'garden of solitude' where the true self comes forward and flourishes" in his presence.[8]

LISTEN FOR HIS VOICE: 1

DELIGHT IN MY WORDS

*Read and reflect on these verses of Scripture
and the letter from your Abba that follows.*

Blessed is the man
    who does not walk in the counsel of the wicked
or stand in the way of sinners
    or sit in the seat of mockers.
But his delight is in the law of the LORD,
    and on his law he meditates day and night.
He is like a tree planted by streams of water,
    which yields its fruit in season
and whose leaf does not wither.
Whatever he does prospers. PS. 1:1–3 NIV

Dear Child,

The generation you live in is full of cynics who mock what is lovely and doubt what is true. They speak empty words they call "wisdom." But I am asking you to turn from their philosophy and live in a different way. I am calling you to delight in me. To know my voice and delight in my words. To stand with people of hope rather than with people of despair. To trust my promises rather than their proclamations of doom. For as you hear my words in your heart, as you meditate day and night upon them in your spirit, you will grow strong. Cynics will always be restless and driven. They will look for light and not find it. They will thirst for peace and not be satisfied. But you will be like a tree planted by streams of water. Your thirst will be quenched. Your branches will be strong, and the fruit of your life will be rich and plentiful.

> *Delight in my words,*
> *Abba*

WRITE A LETTER TO YOUR ABBA: 1

PRAYERS OF LISTENING

*After reading and reflecting on God's words to you, write your own letter
to him in your journal or in the space below, using the following guide:*

1. In your letter to Abba God, tell him about the messages you hear from
   the world around you that conflict with what he is telling you. Are they
   messages of fear—fear of not having enough, fear of growing old or
   dying, fear of being alone? Or are they messages of self-sufficiency
   telling you that you must struggle to meet all of your own needs? Ask
   God to reveal in you one negative worldly message. Ask him to help
   you find a Scripture verse to refute that message.

   Dear Abba,

   _____

   _____

   _____

2. Now put down your pen. Ask Abba to speak to you. Sit quietly for ten
   minutes (or more) and listen to him in your heart. What is he saying to
   you about concentrating on his life-giving messages? What personal
   words of love, guidance, or challenge do you hear? Write these out in
   your journal. (Remember, God's word in your heart will never conflict
   with his revealed Word in the Bible.)

   CLOSING PRAYER: *Dear Abba, thank you so much for the gift of
   your Word. Thank you for addressing all of our problems, fears, and
   misconceptions with your words of truth. Continue to open my heart to
   your Word and my life to your Word Incarnate, Jesus Christ. In his name,
   Amen.*

LISTEN FOR HIS VOICE: 2

LET THE WORDS OF JESUS
CHANGE YOU

Now when he saw the crowds, he went up on a mountainside and sat down. His disciples came to him, and he began to teach them. MATT. 5:1–2 NIV

When Jesus had finished saying these things, the crowds were amazed at his teaching, because he taught as one who had authority, and not as their teachers of the law. MATT. 7:28–29 NIV

My Child,

To the one who knows my Son, his words will be more than words. They will become the open door to a changed life. For they have the power to penetrate, to shape, to realign the character. His words are sometimes uncomfortable, even painful, for they challenge every cherished affection and uproot every buried prejudice. They reveal in the one who is willing to see it a need for change so deep that no amount of self-effort will ever be enough. And when you recognize that need in yourself, my child, draw near to Jesus. Open your heart and let the work of his spirit begin in you. In his presence you will hear other words—words of healing and hope and restoration. And his love will make you new.

Let his words change you,
Abba

WRITE A LETTER TO YOUR ABBA: 2

PRAYERS OF LISTENING

1. Pick up your Bible and begin to read in any of the following chapters: Matthew 5, 6, 7 or John 14, 15, 16, 17. When you come to a verse that stirs your spirit, stop there. Write that verse in your journal or in the space below and ask Abba God to "unpack" its meaning for you. Write out what he shows you.

Dear Abba,

_____

_____

_____

_____

_____

_____

_____

_____

2. Now put down your pen. Ask Abba to speak to you. Sit quietly for ten minutes (or more) and listen to him in your heart. What is he saying to you about the verse you wrote down? What personal words of encouragement, love, guidance, or challenge do you hear? Write these out in your journal. (Remember, God's word in your heart will never conflict with his revealed Word in the Bible.)

CLOSING PRAYER: *Dear Abba, I tend to resist change and even fear it at times, and yet I know I need it. Thank you for the teaching of your Son, Jesus, and how it changes me. I choose to open my spirit to his words today and allow them to do their work in me. Amen.*

LISTEN FOR HIS VOICE: 3
LISTEN FOR MY WORDS OF LIFE

How sweet are your words to my taste,
sweeter than honey to my mouth! Ps. 119:103 NIV

Lord, to whom shall we go? You have the words of eternal life. JOHN
6:68 NIV

My Child,

*I will pose a question to you. How would you feel if you went to lunch
with a close friend and that friend did all the talking, never allowing you
to say a word? Sometimes that is how I feel. Don't you see? Ours is a love
relationship in which each of us should speak and each of us should listen.
When you come to me, you should bring me your words, but you should
also bring me your appetite for my words. I have many words to share
with you—words of healing, words of life. So when you come to me, my
child, pour out your heart, and I will listen. Then be still and listen
prayerfully. That is when you will surely hear the silent words my
Spirit speaks.*

Lovingly,
Abba

WRITE A LETTER TO YOUR ABBA: 3
PRAYERS OF LISTENING

1. Picture yourself waiting to meet Jesus in a beautiful setting—seated under a huge oak tree by a stream or on a mountaintop. As he comes toward you, realize that all the words and questions you had for him are being blown away in the cool breeze. All that is left is your desire to hear him speak to you. Write about this scene in your journal or in the space below. What happens when he comes to you? What does he say? Thank Abba God for those words.

Dear Abba,

_____

_____

_____

_____

_____

2. Now put down your pen. Ask Abba to speak to you. Sit quietly for ten minutes (or more) and listen to him in your heart. What is he saying to you about his desire to speak to you? What personal words of love, guidance, or challenge do you hear? Write these out in your journal. (Remember, God's word in your heart will never conflict with his revealed Word in the Bible.)

CLOSING PRAYER: *Dear Abba, forgive me for always being the one who does the talking in my prayer time. I realize that what you have to say to me is vital. Help me to listen and to hear. And thank you, Father, for always being there to hear me. Amen.*

LISTEN FOR HIS VOICE: 4

MY WORDS ARE FOR TODAY

Do not think that I have come to abolish the Law or the Prophets; I have not come to abolish them but to fulfill them. I tell you the truth, until heaven and earth disappear, not the smallest letter, not the least stroke of a pen, will by any means disappear from the Law until everything is accomplished. Anyone who breaks one of the least of these commandments and teaches others to do the same will be called least in the kingdom of heaven, but whoever practices and teaches these commands will be called great in the kingdom of heaven. For I tell you that unless your righteousness surpasses that of the Pharisees and the teachers of the law, you will certainly not enter the kingdom of heaven. MATT. 5:17–20 NIV

My Child,

Some may try to tell you my words are outdated. That was for another day, they say, but this is a modern age with different needs and standards. Please hear what I am saying to you now if you wish to live in peace, if you wish to walk in confidence. My words are for all time. Earth may melt or freeze or evaporate. Heaven itself may come to an end. But my words will never disappear. Never! Not one letter. Not the dot of one i. My words are as constant as my character. They are the same yesterday, today, and forever. Whoever listens for my words will be strengthened and enriched. And whoever knows and trusts my Son, in whom my words are fulfilled, will dwell in me forever.

Everlastingly,
Abba

WRITE A LETTER TO YOUR ABBA: 4

PRAYERS OF LISTENING

1. In your letter to Abba God, tell him where you need the guidance of his word in your life. Be specific. For instance, don't just say "in my relationships," say, "Show me how to be a better parent."

Dear Abba,

_____

_____

_____

_____

_____

_____

_____

_____

_____

_____

_____

_____

2. Now put down your pen. Ask Abba to speak to you. Sit quietly for ten minutes (or more) and listen to him in your heart. What is he saying to you about the importance and the relevance of his Word? What personal words of love, guidance, or challenge do you hear? Write these out in your journal. (Remember, God's word in your heart will never conflict with his revealed Word in the Bible.)

CLOSING PRAYER: *Dear Abba, help me to be a seeker of your truth. Help me to honor your Word by studying it. Help me to uphold its authority in my life by the way I live. Continue to speak to me, Lord, as I continue to seek your answers in your Word. Amen.*

LISTEN FOR HIS VOICE: 5

FOCUS ON THE LASTING THINGS

He came to a village where a woman named Martha opened her home to him. She had a sister called Mary, who sat at the Lord's feet listening to what he said. But Martha was distracted by all the preparations that had to be made. She came to him and asked, "Lord, don't you care that my sister has left me to do the work by myself? . . ."

"Martha, Martha," the Lord answered, "you are worried and upset about many things, but only one thing is needed. Mary has chosen what is better, and it will not be taken away from her." LUKE 10:38–42 NIV

My Child,

The world could end today. If it did, would your heart be focused on the important, lasting thing, or would you be caught up in the transient trivia upon which this world sets its focus?

"What is lasting? What is important?" you ask me. Mary understood what Martha did not grasp. While Martha busied herself with "many things," Mary sat in the presence of my Son and listened to his words. Oh, my child, is it so difficult to understand? The important, lasting thing is for you to spend time in his presence and in mine! This time spent on lasting things is all you can take with you when this world has faded. It is all that really matters when the assets and liabilities of this world have been tallied. It is the food that fills your emptiness and the living water that quenches your inner thirst.

Be hungry and thirsty for me,
Your Abba

WRITE A LETTER TO YOUR ABBA: 5

PRAYERS OF LISTENING

1. In your letter to Abba God, tell him some of the things you have been preoccupied with lately that you know are not the best use of your time. Weigh the importance of each, comparing it with the importance of spending time with him. If God leads you to this conclusion, write these words beside each thing you have listed: "Time spent with you is more important."

Dear Abba,

_____

_____

_____

_____

_____

_____

2. Now put down your pen. Ask Abba God to speak to you. Then sit quietly for ten minutes (or more) and listen to him in your heart. What is he saying to you today about focusing on lasting things? What personal words of love, guidance, or challenge do you hear? Write these out in your journal. (Remember, God's word in your heart will never contradict his revealed Word in the Bible.)

CLOSING PRAYER: *Dear Abba, forgive me when my days are crowded with "many things." Forgive me when my energy and attention are focused on the outer trappings of life. I want to be like Mary and choose the better part. Strengthen me in my decision to spend more time in your presence. Amen.*

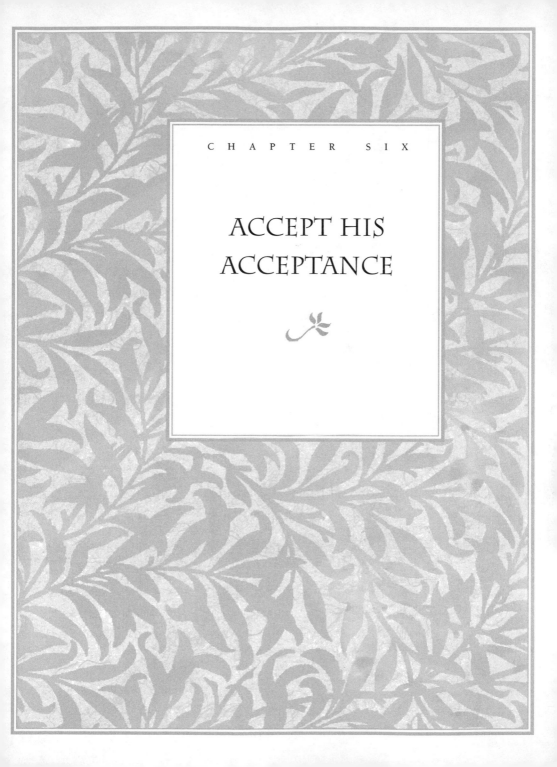

CHAPTER SIX

ACCEPT HIS ACCEPTANCE

ACCEPT HIS ACCEPTANCE

My friend Samantha sighed wearily. "I feel drained," she said.

"Well, that's understandable," I countered, patting her three-month-old cherub, Allison, who was sleeping snugly in the infant seat between us.

"No," Samantha corrected me, "not that kind of drained. Emotionally drained. I've been thinking and praying about it, and I know what it is. I'm just plain exhausted from trying to be good enough. I'm worn out from trying to win my parents' approval. At some level I know they must love me. They say they do. They have always been there for me. But somehow I don't feel loved. When I strip away all the words and birthday presents and outward expressions, I have this feeling in the pit of my stomach that there is something more I have to do to earn a place for myself in their hearts."

A VAGUE FEELING OF UNWORTHINESS

I wonder how many of us walk around day after day with that same nagging feeling that there is something more we must do to justify our existence to ourselves, to our loved ones, or perhaps even to God.

That feeling of being not-quite-okay, vaguely unworthy, somehow unacceptable, is not uncommon. It is the feeling that advertisers capitalize on to sell us their products.

"With this car, this furniture, this new face cream, or this cologne," they tell us, "you will finally have the stamp of approval you need from others." "If you can only get your glassware free of spots, your lawn free of weeds, your carpet free of lint," they promise, "you'll finally be found lovable."

And so we earn more degrees, more merit badges, more money, to prove our value. We do more charitable work, meet more civic responsibilities, work in more prestigious church positions. We have our houses remodeled, our faces lifted, our tummies tucked. But somehow we cannot quiet the voice inside that tells us we aren't quite making the grade.

Henri Nouwen, in his book *Life of the Beloved,* observed that the greatest pitfall in modern life is not success, popularity, or power, but self-rejection.

> When we have come to believe in the voices that call us worthless and unlovable, then success, popularity and power are easily perceived as attractive solutions. The real trap, however, is self-rejection. . . . Self-rejection is the greatest enemy of the spiritual life because it contradicts the sacred voice that calls us the "Beloved."[1]

UNMET NEEDS AND INNER HEALING

Like Samantha, most of us who struggle with feelings of unworthiness or self-rejection can trace those feelings to unmet needs of childhood. It doesn't take a monstrous child abuser to render a child poverty stricken in the area of self-esteem. A well-intending parent who is unable to make positive eye contact or give meaningful touch or verbal affirmation can produce low self-esteem in his or her child without ever intending to. Tragic circumstances, such as the death of one parent or a divorce, may rob a child of uninterrupted parental nurture, thus producing in the child feelings of rejection.

In this fallen world there are no perfect family situations, but God holds out healing for our childhood wounds. He uses those wounds as gateways to the inner work he wants to do. The "gaping holes in people's souls are what God so yearns to gain admittance to, into which he longs to pour His healing life."[2]

The Messages That Speak Acceptance

As we allow the affirming words of God's love to define us, we will be healed. What are the messages that heal and define us and lead us to accept his acceptance? The message I heard first from the Father was the one I needed most.

"I KNOW YOU"

From the time I was able to talk, I was known in my family as an actress and a dreamer. My Aunt Nyada called me "Dreamboat," and my parents fluctuated between trying to help me face reality and trying to help me put all of my drama and dreaminess to some constructive use. It took me years to recognize the downside to always acting a role: It's easy to lose touch with who you really are.

As a young wife, I had dreamed of sharing the intimate communication of a marriage relationship. But I was constantly shifting from role to role, unable to be "my real self" with my husband because I didn't *know* my real self. And perhaps because he wasn't sure exactly who he was dealing with from day to day, he was unable or unwilling to be vulnerable with me.

Finally, as our communication grew more and more threadbare, as our marriage grew more and more shaky, I could see that we were losing each other. There was no dreaming or acting my way out of this one. I needed something real, Someone real. I needed God.

On a cold January night as I sat up until nearly dawn trying to find the courage to put my life into his hands, I came across this verse: "Delight yourself in the LORD, and he will give you the desires of your heart" (Ps. 37:4 NIV).

"But that's just the problem," I said to him. "I don't even *know* the desires of my heart. If an angel in a solid gold halo appeared to me, offering to grant me anything my heart desired, I wouldn't know what to ask for."

But I know the desires of your heart, was the Lord's silent reply. *You see, I know you. I made you. And I am the only One who knows what will satisfy you at the core of who you are.*

That night I found what I had been looking for all my life—the

One who sees through every mask and disguise. The One who truly knows me.

Joanie's Story

Several years ago at a women's retreat I prayed with a vivacious young woman I'll call Joanie, who confessed to me her deep yearning to be truly known. Joanie, the wife of a successful pastor and the mother of four beautiful daughters, was attractive and talented. To see her on the outside, you would never know she lacked anything, but inside, Joanie was hurting.

"Claire," she said, fighting back the tears, "it's so hard to be a pastor's wife. There's no one I can be real with—no one but Jack, and he's so tired, I hate to burden him with one more thing. The church doesn't care about me—not really. They just want someone they can wind up like a robot who'll come out baking casseroles and chairing the women's ministry. A couple of Sundays ago, a woman came up to me after the service and said, 'Pastor Jack talks about you so much in his sermons, I feel like I know you!' I wanted to scream, 'But you don't know me! You don't know the first thing about me!'" Joanie began to sob. "I need someplace where I can be known and appreciated for myself."

As I prayed for Joanie, I realized she was filled with anger toward her husband's new congregation. And that anger was keeping her from the healing she needed. She needed to forgive those who had been unwilling to see her for herself and unable to meet her needs.

"Only one Person knows you completely, and only he can fully meet your needs," I reminded her.

That night Joanie chose to let go of her anger and forgive "the church people." She agreed to begin listening for God's affirming words, allowing him to show her who she is in Christ.

Several months after our time of prayer, I got a letter from Joanie in which she said, "The Lord has showed me that I was partly to blame for keeping myself locked in the role of pastor's wife. I was afraid of not being accepted for myself. The more I feel the Lord's acceptance, the more willing I am to risk being me. And I am finally making some friends."

Wherever you are today, however carefully you may have tried to hide your heart, God the Father sees your hidden wounds, your unspoken feelings and needs. Like a friend, he longs to speak intimate words of acceptance to you. If you listen, you will hear him saying, "I know you. I love you. I will meet your needs."

"I HAVE WONDERFUL PLANS FOR YOUR LIFE!"

Sometimes feelings of self-rejection grow out of a sense of uselessness. We may feel that we have no gifts, no talents, no particular "call" on our lives. We look at others whose gifts are widely acclaimed, who seem to be achieving great things for the kingdom of God, and we feel like spiritual afterthoughts—unwanted stepchildren. *How could God ever use us?* we may wonder.

The longer I know the Lord, the more convinced I am of this one thing: God's love is not random or haphazard. It's not just some sloppy-agape feel-good experience. There is reason and purpose behind everything. There is a design for every life.

In Jeremiah 29:11, God tells his people, "I know the plans I have for you, . . . plans to prosper you and not to harm you, plans to give you hope and a future" (NIV).

Those are beautiful words to me. I have learned the hard way that my own plans (however good they may look or feel to me) are not what I'm here for (see Prov. 16:25). I believe it takes falling flat on our faces spiritually a few times before we finally realize that God designed us for his plans and purposes, and they are the only ones that will make us truly happy.

Ephesians 3:20 says that Jesus is able to do "much, much more than anything we can ask or imagine." What this means to me is that he wants to bless me with better things than I can even think up to ask him for. He knows what I need and what will satisfy me.

Sometimes, though, it's hard to keep his purposes in focus when the world puts forth such a different perspective. I recently attended one of those "black-balloon" birthday parties where all of the cards and jokes centered around the honoree being "over the hill." Even though everything was said in a light, good-natured manner, before long I could feel a heaviness in the air. I realized we were joking about something that our youth-obsessed culture tries to push as truth—the idea that life and joy and plans for the future are only for the young.

The real truth is that we Christians should have a rainbow-colored assortment of balloons at every birthday party, because we follow a God who has important plans for us, whatever our age!

God's Timeless and Tailor-Made Purposes

Mary was only a teenager when she made her journey to Bethlehem and gave birth to her very special Child. But Abraham and Sarah had celebrated many decades of "black-balloon birthdays" by the time God's little surprise package, Isaac, arrived in their lives. Both births were crucial to God's plan.

David was just a boy with a slingshot when he brought down Goliath and saved his country. Moses, on the other hand, began the biggest journey of his career in his eightieth year. God has big plans for each one of us whatever our age.

And it's not only Bible-era characters who testify to God's timeless purposes in our lives. Modern-era saints both young and old still discover God's plans when they are willing to open their lives to his voice and his vision. Loren Cunningham was a very young man when he envisioned an army of young people moving in waves over the globe taking the message of Christ to the whole world. That vision became Youth with a Mission, the interdenominational youth missionary organization that has sent millions of young Christian missionaries all over the world since its inception.

Corrie ten Boom's missionary journey, on the other hand, did not begin until she was fifty-six years old. Corrie left the horrors of confinement in Ravensbruck, a Nazi prison camp, to keep a promise she had made there to her sister, Betsie—a promise to tell the world that there is no darkness so deep that God's love is not deeper still. And though Corrie's ministry did not begin until her mid-fifties, it lasted for nearly thirty years!

Our God still comes to us today as he did to Mary, to Moses, to

Corrie, in unexpected places speaking surprising words, drawing us into exciting, challenging circumstances. He still breaks the bread of everyday life and hands it back to us as joy and purpose and deep fulfillment of the heart.

"YOU ARE MY FAVORITE"

Several months ago I got to sit in on a Sunday school class that our son, Curt, was teaching, and I learned something about who I am in Christ—something I will never forget.

Curt said he had been listening for God's still, small voice one morning in his prayer time when he heard God say to him, *Curt, you are my favorite.*

"I must have heard that wrong," Curt thought. "How can I be God's favorite? God's favorite is in first place. He is at the top of the heap in God's estimation. Moses was God's favorite. David was God's favorite. Jesus is God's favorite. But me? Surely not!"

Wondering what in the world God was trying to say to him, he opened his dictionary and looked up the word *favorite.* The definition read, "A person or thing regarded with special favor or preference."

"Okay, I see, Father," Curt prayed, feeling that he now understood. "I am *one of* your favored ones. Thank you, Father."

No, Curt, God's voice said insistently in his Spirit. *It's more than that. You are my favorite. You are number one in my heart. If you had been the only one on earth, I would have sent Jesus to die just for you. If you were the only one trusting me today, I would carry on with my plan just for you. Curt, you are my favorite!*

As I heard Curt's words, I knew that I, too, am God's favorite. And so are you. For this is the mind-blowing reality of my faith: I serve a God who is able to love me as though I were his only child.

Anabel's Story

Author and teacher Anabel Gillham, like Curt, had never thought of herself as a personal favorite of God's. Being a "performance-based person," she could believe John 3:16 for "us," the great masses of humanity, but she could not believe that *she* had done anything spectacular enough to earn God's special attention. She saw herself as "simply one among the millions, an unknown secret admirer with an autographed photo."

Then one day, as Anabel was preparing to send her beloved son, Mason, a profoundly retarded little boy, back to the state school for retarded children, God showed her something that would change her life forever.

Kneeling by her son's chair, struggling with the heart-wrenching task of saying good-bye, she took his hands in hers and said, "Mason, I love you. I love you. If only you could understand how much I love you." How she longed to know that her little boy understood, but, as always, Mason just stared.

In that emotional moment God spoke to Anabel: "Anabel, you don't look at your son and turn away in disgust because he's sitting there with saliva drooling out of his mouth. . . . You don't reject Mason . . . because he doesn't perform for you. You love him, Anabel, just because he is yours. Mason doesn't willfully reject your love, but you willfully reject Mine. I love you, Anabel, not because you perform for me, but just because you're Mine." It was as though spiritual light bulbs flashed in that moment. Suddenly Anabel understood that she didn't have to do anything for God to win his love. She only had to see herself as his favored and "favorite" child. She only had to accept his acceptance.[3]

"SEE YOURSELF THROUGH MY EYES"

I believe that if we could ever get a God's-eye view of ourselves, we would find it so much easier to accept his acceptance. We would see ourselves as one of a kind, unique creations designed by the One who takes pride in his workmanship.

Years ago the Father gave me a wonderful glimpse of how tenderly he views us, his children. That year we made one of many mistakes in our parenting career—we bought a car for our two sons who were then teenagers.

It was a real jalopy—a well-worn, faded-silver AMC Spirit. We always referred to that car as "the Spirit." In fact, we often responded to their requests to go out by saying, "Yes, you may go tonight, if the Spirit moves you!" (Which it frequently did not!)

We began to have trouble with the Spirit before we ever got it in our driveway. The man who had owned it before us had failed to register the car properly, and the papers were in a terrible mess. Thus I was forced to spend one of those maddening days in the courthouse being sent from one wrong waiting line to another.

I think I was in my third wrong line when I realized I had been standing there cold-heartedly plotting a way to strangle the woman behind the desk with her own typewriter ribbon. It was at this juncture that the Lord tapped me on the shoulder and whispered, *See that woman behind the desk?*

"Yes, Lord," I answered.

I love her.

I paused.

"You're kidding!" I finally replied, incredulous at his undiscriminating taste.

I'm not kidding, he insisted. *Try seeing her through my eyes.*

"Well, since I'm going to be here until Jesus comes back anyway, I might as well try," I said.

Then, as I looked at the nondescript little gray-haired typing clerk behind the desk, something amazing began to take place. I began to see wonderful things about her that I had not noticed even moments before. There was a dimple at the top of each finger, just like a baby might have. I loved those dimples! Her eyebrows were like tiny teepees that rose above her glasses in perfect points. *Precious,* I thought. Her hair moved across her head in obviously natural waves that rose and fell and rose and fell in perfect symmetry. *How lovely she is,* I found myself thinking.

And, what I think I loved best of all was a framed cartoon of a little clown, typing, that hung behind her desk. I could just picture her at home each morning dressing to come to this thankless job where people would treat her rudely (as I had just been getting ready to do). And still she had enough humor to think of herself as a little clown. By this time, I loved this woman. I really loved her!

When it was finally my turn in line, I found myself moving toward her desk wearing a warm, loving smile. When she saw that smile, I believe she was confused and a bit overwhelmed. It may have been her first smile of the day.

Then I showed her my automobile papers, and she responded, "You know, don't you, that you're in the wrong line?"

I didn't even frown. I just kept looking at her with what I imagine must have been an expression of amazement over how much I cared for her.

"Why don't you wait here," she suddenly volunteered, "and let me see if I can take care of this for you." When she returned, she explained that the error had been cleared up and all I'd have to do was pay my fees downstairs.

"How wonderful of you!" I said. "Thank you so much!"

Then she did the oddest thing. She stood up and walked me to the door. I honestly think she hated to see me go. We almost embraced! I was missing her already.

Very sincerely, she put her hand on my arm and said, "Please let me know if I can ever do anything to help you."

I walked out into the hall totally shaken by what I had just experienced. A miracle had just taken place in the Mobile County Courthouse.

"What was that, Lord?" I asked him. "What *was* that?"

That, he replied, *was my love for that typing clerk coming to her through you, and it blew her away. Do you see now how much I love my children—how much love and pride I take in each one of them?*

"YOU ARE MY BELOVED CHILD"

If we are ever to fully accept our God's acceptance, we must know more than who we are. We must know *whose* we are.

We must hear the sacred voice at the center of ourselves, the voice of our Abba, saying, "You are my beloved child, my own. I formed you in your mother's womb. I have known you from before the foundation of the world. You are unique and precious to me."

The blessed ones who have heard and received those words of affirmation and acceptance know a peace that the world cannot counterfeit. They have nothing to prove. They are drawn by the flame of love rather than driven by the whip of competition. They are at home in their Father's universe as small children are at home in their own backyards. Friendship with their Abba is their daily bread; the inner whisper of his still, small voice is the music they dance to; the breeze on their faces is the kiss of his Holy Spirit. And prayer is the pure, sweet atmosphere in which they breathe.

Norman's Story

Nearly twenty years ago I was blessed to meet a man named Norman Grubb who understood his "beloved child" status perhaps better than anyone I have ever known. Norman, who was in his late seventies then, was an English gentleman in every sense of the word, with silvery-white hair, rosy cheeks, and a twinkle in his clear, blue eyes.

Norman was well known in the Christian world for having been a founding member of the Worldwide Evangelism Crusade in England (now WEC International), and he was the author of more than thirty books, yet he never felt the need to impress anyone with his accomplishments. He was always humble and gracious. Whatever was set before him at mealtime, he pronounced it "Lovely!" and ate it with gusto. Whatever bedroom he was assigned to, he acted as though he'd been given the keys to the Taj Mahal. And though his clothes were often worn, I never once heard him ask for money from a congregation or a Christian gathering. He trusted God completely for every provision.

Once when Norman was staying with us, he got a cold that became bronchitis, and I grew quite concerned for his health. He was, after all, almost ninety years old at the time!

"Norman," I asked him one late night when his cough seemed to be getting worse, "don't you think I should call the doctor or take you to the hospital?"

He smiled the most peaceful and radiant smile. "Oh, my darling," he answered in his lovely English accent, "you go back to bed now. All is well. I am held in the most loving hands."

Though Norman preached well into his nineties, his health finally began to fail. He was ninety-eight years old when we received our last letter from him, in which he counted his blessings and recalled with great thanksgiving the day that "Jesus revealed Himself to me as my personal savior in 1914."

Less than a year later, we heard from Norman's grandson, Daniel, who told us of his grandfather's home-going: "Norman had no pain in his final hours. . . . [Though] his voice was too weak for words, . . . he was able to verbalize his last cry, 'Abba, Abba—please take me, please take me.'" Norman's mission here on earth was complete.

He was ready for the home he was going to and confident of the arms that were waiting for him there.

Into the envelope, Daniel had slipped one of the last snapshots ever taken of Norman. He was sitting up in bed, wearing a huge smile and a T-shirt that bore the words FAITH LAUGHS AT ADVERSITY.

Norman Grubb was a man who knew he was God's "beloved child." He had long ago accepted his Father's acceptance and had learned to live out his life day by day as a vessel containing the Spirit of Jesus.

HIS PART AND OUR PART

Our Father is extending his acceptance to all of us, his children, but he will not force it on us. It is our part to receive it. It is our responsibility to possess our possessions.

When I was in my late twenties I had to possess my possessions in a very literal sense. I learned that in my Great-Aunt Edith's will her antique furniture had been left to me. Naturally, I was very excited! But my excitement did little toward putting me in possession of my inheritance. I had to hire a moving company to back up a truck to her quaint, old Victorian house, to load the furniture aboard, and to deliver it to my home in another town before it could actually be mine.

Accepting God's acceptance is like that. His part is to speak his words of love to us. Words that let us know he knows us and values us. Words that tell of his plans for our lives and of our favor in his sight. Words that assure us we are thoroughly unique and totally beloved. His part is to speak the words. Our part is to draw near and hear them—to take them in and digest them, for it is by his words of acceptance that we learn to live as his children.

ACCEPT HIS ACCEPTANCE: 1
COME KNOW THE JOY
OF BELONGING

Read and reflect on these verses of Scripture
and the letter from your Abba that follows.

When the kindness and love of God our Savior was shown, he saved us because of his mercy. It was not because of good deeds we did to be right with him. He saved us through the washing that made us new people through the Holy Spirit. TITUS 3:4–5

You know the grace of our Lord Jesus Christ. You know that Christ was rich, but for you he became poor so that by his becoming poor you might become rich. 2 COR. 8:9

God will show his mercy forever and ever to those who worship and serve him. LUKE 1:50

My Child,

You are rushing around day after day trying to earn my approval and garner my affection. You work so hard trying to look good in my sight. Know this, my child, you are very beautiful in my sight right this minute, not because of your striving to look better, but because I have made you and you are mine. You are loved by me, not because of what you work to achieve, but because of what my Son, Jesus, achieved for you on Calvary. You can only be made right with me by his blood; you can only be made clean in my sight by the washing of my Word and my Spirit. Come and let my mercy and grace pour over you. Then your striving and struggling will melt into the joy of my acceptance. Come know the joy of belonging to me.

Your Father and Friend,
Abba

WRITE A LETTER TO YOUR ABBA: 1

PRAYERS OF WHOLENESS

After reading and reflecting on God's words to you,
write your own letter to him, using the guide below:

1. See yourself as a child coming home from school. Do you kick off your shoes and go to the refrigerator for a snack? Do you put your feet up and relax after a hard day? Or are you forced to behave like a guest in your own home, always on your best behavior, always trying to earn the approval of your parents? In your letter to Abba God, reflect on what your own home was like while you were growing up. Now consider your Abba's love, and picture yourself coming home to his house. Describe it in your journal or in the space below.

Dear Abba,

_____

_____

_____

2. Now put down your pen. Ask Abba to speak to you. Sit quietly for ten minutes (or more) and listen to him in your heart. What is he saying to you about his acceptance of you? What personal words of love, guidance, or challenge do you hear? Write these out in your journal. (Remember, God's word in your heart will never conflict with his revealed Word in the Bible.)

CLOSING PRAYER: *Dear Abba, thank you for the grace of Jesus that has opened the front door of your acceptance to me. Thank you for his love that encircles me, for his blood that cleanses me, for his mercy that befriends me so that I can stand in your presence as your own. Amen.*

ACCEPT HIS ACCEPTANCE: 2

FOLLOW MY LEAD

The LORD your God is with you; the mighty One will save you. He will rejoice over you. You will rest in his love; he will sing and be joyful about you. ZEPH. 3:17

So you will go out with joy
and be led out in peace.
The mountains and hills will burst into song before you,
and all the trees in the fields will clap their hands.
ISA. 55:12

My Child,

You are my favorite. I have chosen you. Come, enter into this spiritual "dance" with me—the dance of acceptance. Let me show you how to follow my lead, how to move in response to every slight pressure of my Holy Spirit, feeling the rhythm of my heartbeat and following the freedom of my love. When you allow my love and mercy to be the background music of your daily life, when you choose to move through each moment as my partner in the dance, you will know the freedom and joy of being my child. Praise will flow out of you like the joyous melody of a familiar song.

Let me lead in your life,
Abba

WRITE A LETTER TO YOUR ABBA: 2
PRAYERS OF WHOLENESS

1. In your letter to Abba God, accept his invitation to the dance of acceptance. Tell him what his acceptance means to you.

Dear Abba,

_____

_____

_____

_____

_____

_____

_____

_____

_____

_____

2. Now put down your pen. Ask Abba to speak to you. Sit quietly for ten minutes (or more) and listen to him in your heart. What is he saying to you about the joy of being accepted? What personal words of love, guidance, or challenge do you hear? Write these out in your journal. (Remember, God's word in your heart will never conflict with his revealed Word in the Bible.)

CLOSING PRAYER: *Dear Abba, help me to hear your still, small voice which is constantly inviting me to follow you in the "dance of acceptance." Help me hear the music, and help me to follow your lead. I love you, Lord. Amen.*

ACCEPT HIS ACCEPTANCE: 3

I MADE YOU AS YOU ARE

You made my whole being;
  you formed me in my mother's body.
I praise you because you made me in an amazing
  and wonderful way. Ps. 139:13–14

God has made us what we are. In Christ Jesus, God made us to do good works, which God planned in advance for us to live our lives doing. Eph. 2:10

Dear Child,

My love for you has a plan and a purpose behind it. I labored over you with the skill and care of a craftsman who designs a beautiful piece of furniture. He plans the size and style of his creation to meet a need in the household. He carefully crafts the drawers to slide in and out smoothly, for he is aware of what they will contain. He knows the precise corner of the room where his masterpiece will fit. He can picture the way the morning sunlight will slant through the window and fall upon the polished grain of the wood. I designed you exactly as you are to fill a space in my heart and in my household. It is a space that no one else can fill. I created you with your precise gifts and abilities to fill a role in my kingdom that is tailor-made for you. Today you may not have the vaguest notion of what my purposes are, but I am asking you to believe that my plans for you are good. They will bring you deep meaning and fulfillment. If you trust me, I will help you find them.

I am the Craftsman,
Abba

WRITE A LETTER TO YOUR ABBA: 3
PRAYERS OF WHOLENESS

1. In your letter, ask Abba God to help you see yourself as his "masterpiece." Ask him to begin revealing to you his plans and purposes.

Dear Abba,

_____

_____

_____

_____

_____

_____

_____

_____

_____

_____

2. Now put down your pen. Ask Abba God to speak to you. Sit quietly for ten minutes (or more) and listen for him in your heart. What is he saying to you about his plans for you? What personal words of love, guidance, or challenge do you hear? Write these out in your journal. (Remember, God's word in your heart will never conflict with his revealed Word in the Bible.)

CLOSING PRAYER: *Dear Abba, thank you for the careful way you designed me. Thank you for the promise that you hold a good future and a bright hope for me. Help me to seek your plans for me, and when I find them, help me to follow. Amen.*

ACCEPT HIS ACCEPTANCE: 4

IT'S YOU I WANT

Brothers and sisters, look at what you were when God called you. Not many of you were wise in the way the world judges wisdom. Not many of you had great influence. Not many of you came from important families. But God chose the foolish things of the world to shame the wise, and he chose the weak things of the world to shame the strong. He chose what the world thinks is unimportant and what the world looks down on and thinks is nothing in order to destroy what the world thinks is important. God did this so that no one can brag in his presence. Because of God you are in Christ Jesus, who has become for us wisdom from God. In Christ we are put right with God, and have been made holy, and have been set free from sin. 1 COR. 1:26–30

My Dear Child,

By the world's criteria, you may have judged yourself unkindly at times. You may have felt that you didn't measure up—that you lacked the brains or the looks or the connections needed to "move in the right circles." Well, I do not require that you earn another degree or land a better job or join some prestigious private club before you are acceptable to me. I have called you to be mine right where you are because you are exactly the person I want on my team. Let the world use its standards, and I will use mine. When I chose you to be mine, I knew very well what I was doing. I see tremendous value in you that may never be applauded by the world. But in Christ, equipped with his wisdom and vision and humility, you will be a spiritual powerhouse for me! Watch out world!

I am proud of you!
Abba

WRITE A LETTER TO YOUR ABBA: 4
PRAYERS OF WHOLENESS

1. In your letter to Abba God, tell him of times you have longed to "fit in" but instead have felt like a misfit. Thank him for ways that he is helping you see your value.

Dear Abba,

_____

_____

_____

_____

_____

_____

_____

_____

_____

_____

_____

2. Now put down your pen. Ask Abba to speak to you. Sit quietly for ten minutes (or more) and listen to him in your heart. What is he saying to you about who you are in him? What personal words of love, guidance, or challenge do you hear? Write these out in your journal. (Remember, God's word in your heart will never conflict with his revealed Word in the Bible.)

CLOSING PRAYER: *Dear Abba, I am so grateful that you can see in me what the world may never see. Give me a vision of who you have designed me to be and give me the faith to follow you to the fulfillment of that vision. Thank you for loving me. Amen.*

ACCEPT HIS ACCEPTANCE: 5

MAKE PEACE WITH WHO YOU ARE

Peace I leave with you; my peace I give you. I do not give to you as the world gives. Do not let your hearts be troubled and do not be afraid. JOHN 14:27 NIV

Oh, My Precious Child,

There is someone you need to make peace with. Someone who needs your friendship and acceptance. Do you have any idea who I am talking about? I am talking about you, yourself. I accept you as you are. Can you not accept yourself? Must you be your own worst enemy—your own most severe critic? I am certain you would never judge others as harshly as you judge yourself or treat others as uncharitably as you treat yourself. If Jesus has given his own life for your freedom and I have embraced you as my own child, isn't it time that you looked upon yourself with some kindness? Isn't it time that you made peace with yourself, my child? I delight in you just as you are. You are who I designed you to be. Make peace with your looks, your voice, your gifts, your personality. Be yourself. Be mine. Be at peace.

> *I love you,*
> *Abba*

WRITE A LETTER TO YOUR ABBA: 5
PRAYERS OF WHOLENESS

1. In your imagination, see yourself standing before a judge. He is Jesus Christ. He lifts his gavel and pronounces his judgment: "Not guilty!" He proclaims his sentence: "Freedom!" As you rise to leave the courtroom, a free person, you notice that behind his bench, there is a cross, and you suddenly understand his verdict. In your letter to Abba God, tell him what this scene means to you.

Dear Abba,

_____

_____

_____

_____

_____

2. Now put down your pen. Ask Abba to speak to you. Sit quietly for ten minutes (or more) and listen to him in your heart. What is he saying to you about making peace with who you are? What personal words of encouragement, love, guidance, or challenge do you hear? Write these out in your journal. (Remember, God's word in your heart will never conflict with his revealed Word in the Bible.)

CLOSING PRAYER: *Dear Abba, I confess to you that it is easier for me to forgive and be at peace with others than it is to forgive and be at peace with myself. Thank you for the Cross of Calvary and what Jesus did for me there. Help me to receive your forgiveness and your acceptance. Help me to make peace with myself so that I may be at peace with you and with others. In Jesus' name, Amen.*

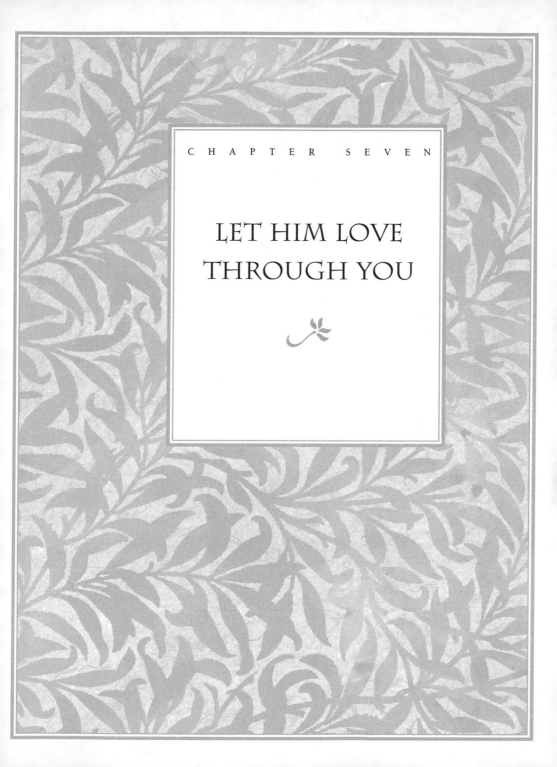

CHAPTER SEVEN

LET HIM LOVE
THROUGH YOU

LET HIM LOVE THROUGH YOU

For years our family enjoyed watching reruns of the *Andy Griffith Show*. One of our favorite episodes is the one in which Sheriff Andy Taylor's skinny, goggle-eyed deputy, Barney Fife, is acquainting two new prisoners with the rules of the tiny, two-cell Mayberry jail.

Swaggering up and down in front of the "lock-down" area with his usual ludicrous air of self-importance, Barney begins his lecture like this: "Here on 'the Rock' we have two rules. The first rule is— 'obey all rules.'"

Here on the rock we call Planet Earth, things are a little more complicated. We are bombarded with countless rules and miles of red tape from all directions. Even in (perhaps especially in) "the land of the free and the home of the brave" we are told at every turn what we can and can't and must do. But unfortunately, nowhere is the rule-keeping mind-set more alive and kicking than in some segments of the church at large.

My Jewish friend Reb attended a Christian Bible study for about a year. She was so excited about it at first that I had high hopes she would come to know the Lord in a personal relationship.

But after the year was up, she told me, "I thought the Christian life was supposed to be about love, but it seems to be mostly about rule-keeping. I always knew Jews had a rule for everything, but Christians are just about as bad. They've managed to take the Ten Commandments and dissect them into a million little nagging do's and don'ts."

TWO INTERTWINED COMMANDMENTS

Reb is right. The Christian life is supposed to be about love, not rules. Jesus made that clear when he was asked a trick question by a Sadducee, an expert in the law.

"Which command in the law is the most important?" asked the expert.

Without hesitation Jesus answered, "'Love the Lord your God with all your heart, all your soul, and all your mind.' This is the first and most important command. And the second command is like the first. 'Love your neighbor as you love yourself.'" Then Jesus added that all the laws and all the writings of the prophets are distilled and incorporated into these two intertwined commandments: loving God and loving others (see Matt. 22:34–40).

If Jesus in his wisdom and mercy was able to distill his expectations of us into two essential commandments, why do we continue to bog our spirits down in a tangle of niggling do's and don'ts?

I believe it's because loving the way he calls us to love is so all-encompassing that it is far more costly and challenging than keeping a million minor religious mandates. For we are called to love not with human love but with superhuman love—to live not as people live but with the mercy of God.

> You must love each other as I have loved you. (John 13:34)

> Whoever says that he lives in God must live as Jesus lived. (1 John 2:6)

LOVE LIKE JESUS?

Live and love as Jesus did? I can't even conceive of the love it took to walk out his life on earth, much less duplicate it.

I could never have loved enough to leave a great, huge, incredible kingdom filled with light and music and everyone there praising me to be born in a stable as a helpless baby—born to a blue-collar father and a teenage mother.

I could never have loved enough to spend thirty years in total obscurity building furniture with my earthly father, much of that time knowing my real heritage and my ultimate destiny.

I could never have loved enough to hang out for three years with twelve guys who didn't get it—no matter how many times I explained it or how many little stories I told to help them get the point.

I could never have loved enough to stand by and be accused by a mob of pompous religious types, taken into custody and questioned by a second-rate official, and convicted with no evidence, all the while keeping my mouth shut.

I could never have loved enough to be beaten and mocked, spat upon and cursed, dressed up like a clown and paraded down a street of jeering peasants who had no idea I was going through all of this for them.

I could never have loved enough to stretch out my arms on the hard wood of a cross and willingly receive nails into my hands and feet—hands that had set the galaxies in their places, feet that had walked the sands of eternity.

And as I was lifted, and as I hung there, naked and broken and gasping for breath, looking down into the cruel, unfeeling faces of the people who had put me where I was, I could never, never have loved enough to look up to heaven and say, "Father, don't hold this against them. Please, Father, don't punish them for this. Forgive them, Father, for they don't know what they're doing!"

OUT OF MY LEAGUE

I don't know a human being other than Jesus himself who could love like that, do you? That level of sacrificial caring is far out of my league, and out of yours. We have no power to be what God's calling us to be. No power to love. No power to live the Christian life. Only one Person has the power to live the Christian life, and that Person is Jesus himself.

Am I implying here that God is some kind of sadist who gets a kick out of setting us up to fail by requiring a level of behavior that's impossible for us to achieve? Our God is not a sadist! He is a loving Father. And what he requires from us, he desires to do in us and through us. That's the incredible mystery he unfolds in Paul's letters (and in our lives if we'll give him the chance). It's his plan for sharing his glory with his children.

DRIVING TOGETHER

Thinking about God's plan for sharing his glory suddenly put me in mind of something special my dad used to do for me when I was about four years old. Our family had a new car around that time—a shiny maroon sedan—and one of my favorite things in the world was when my Daddy would let me "drive." Would I! That was some thrill for a little girl!

I'd climb into his lap and put my hands on his and off we'd go. Of course, my feet couldn't touch the pedals, and my hands were not really doing the steering, but I was experiencing the joy of joining my dad in something he loved to do. We were driving together! I was sharing his view of the road. I was more than just "along for the ride"; I was participating. I was more than just a passenger; I was behind the wheel!

God the Father invites us to participate with him in reaching his destination. He doesn't need us to get there, but he wants to share with us the joy of this ride we call life. He wants us to see things as he sees them and cooperate with him in the steering of our world toward his perfect purposes.

A SPIRITUAL TRANSACTION

But we cannot make this journey in our own power. Cooperating with God and his purposes, sharing his glory, means allowing Jesus Christ to take our old life of death and sin into himself on the cross so that we can receive in its place his new life of love and power. Only when this spiritual transaction has taken place can we ever hope to live as he lived. Only then can we say with Paul, "I was put to death on the cross with Christ, and I do not live anymore—it is Christ who lives in me. I still live in my body, but I live by faith in the Son of God who loved me and gave himself to save me" (Gal. 2:20).

This is the incredible, hidden mystery, now revealed, that Paul whispers to us across centuries of faith: "God decided to let his people know this rich and glorious secret which he has for all people. This secret is Christ himself, who is in you. He is our only hope for glory" (Col. 1:27).

Jesus is not merely the map to freedom; he *is* that freedom! "Faithful is he that calleth you, who also will do it" (1 Thess. 5:24 KJV). The One who calls me to the Christian life is the One who will live it through me. He comes to live out the power of who he is within the frailty of who I am. He comes to live out his own deity within the walls of my humanity. He puts his whole self at my disposal when I put my whole self at his.

THE MYSTERY FLESHED OUT

To see this mystery fleshed out in a life is to understand what Jesus is able to do when he is given "free reign." Major W. Ian Thomas of England is one such life.

Young Ian asked Jesus into his heart when he was a boy of twelve and was convinced of his call to serve the Lord as a missionary by the age of fifteen. He began immediately to preach at open-air meetings and became active in Crusaders' Union Bible classes and meetings. Soon his young life was a whirlwind of charitable "busyness."

Influenced by a doctor serving in Nigeria, Ian decided that he, too, would like to become a doctor and serve in West Africa, so when the time came, he entered the university. There, in addition to his studies, Ian became a leader in InterVarsity Fellowship, filling every spare moment with ministry. Among other things, he started a slum club for children in the East End of London.

"At the age of nineteen, every moment of my day was packed [so] tightly [that I was] reduced to a state of complete spiritual exhaustion," Major Thomas recalled.

"Then one night in November, that year, just at midnight . . . I got down on my knees before God, and I just wept in sheer despair. I said, 'Oh, God, I know that I am saved. I love Jesus Christ. I am perfectly convinced that I am converted. With all my heart I have wanted to serve Thee. I have tried to my uttermost and I am a hopeless failure!'"

That night Ian Thomas heard a message that he had "never once heard from the lips of men." Through his tears he heard the Lord saying, "You see, for seven years, with utmost sincerity, you have been trying to live for Me, on My behalf, the life that I have been waiting for seven years to live through you." In the space of an hour, the Lord unlocked to Ian Thomas the secret of Spirit living.

"I got up the next morning," recalled Thomas, "to an entirely different Christian life, [though] I had not received one iota more than I had already had for seven years!"

Major Ian Thomas did not become a doctor in West Africa. Instead, step by step, God led him into paths of service and evangelism more exciting than any he could have dreamed of. Gone were the weariness and striving. Gone was the desperate feeling that he must save the whole world by his own efforts. Now he was filled with the One who had been waiting to work through him, and rivers of living water flowed![1]

THE PIPELINE PRINCIPLE

God revealed to Major Thomas what he longs to reveal to each of us: that we are simply human pipelines designed to receive the powerful "living water" of his Son's life so that it may nourish our lives and flow to others (see John 15:5). When this becomes a reality to us, we find ourselves amazingly able to live in this world by the power of Jesus, as Jesus lived in this world by the power of his Father.

Awakened to his love as our life force, his power as our heartbeat, we can actually live without worry or self-condemnation, as he did. And as we learn the secret of cooperating with his purposes while resting in his power, we will find all the love we need to serve and care and forgive flowing through the pipeline of our lives.

On my Christian journey, I have been blessed to see the life of Christ pouring through the lives of many ordinary believers into situations and circumstances that might otherwise have seemed hopeless or unbearable. I want to share with you the stories of just a few.

A Pipeline to Faith

In a culture where faith often seems to be in short supply, my friend Carolyn Greene walks by faith. She has had to. Fifteen years ago her two-and-a-half-year-old son, John, fell into their swimming pool and drowned. Attempts to revive him on the way to the hospital were not successful, but twenty minutes later in the emergency room, he was revived. John had suffered from anoxia (a lack of oxygen to the brain), which resulted in severe neurological damage.

Carolyn's life from that point became one of sacrificial love. Her days were given to caring for John. Five hours a day were spent just feeding him. She exercised him and read to him, changed him, and each night rose several times to turn him so that he would not get bedsores. (Over the years since the accident, with little outside help, Carolyn has continued to care for John in these ways.)

Spiritually, Carolyn's life has been given to prayer. God has guided her to certain experimental treatment programs that have given John some small but vital breakthroughs. For instance, he is now able to communicate with his family by using a "Speak Easy" computer.

Though Carolyn's prayer each day is "be it unto me according to your will," it is not a prayer of fatalism but a prayer of faith. She believes that as God's Spirit is poured out, John could receive a full healing any day, supernaturally or through medical research. But in the meantime she is content to trust God to guide her path and give her the strength she needs daily and hourly, dealing with John's condition just as it is.

John Greene's life is powerfully used by the Lord. Time and again I have heard visitors to our church say how blessed they were by the boy in the wheelchair. And it was through John that his own father, Monroe, came to know the Lord last year.

When Carolyn was asked recently how she does all she does she told the story of a mother cat going into a burning house to save her kittens.

"Even an animal has an instinct to help her child," she observed. "I've definitely had that. But God gives us so much more. *He gives us himself,* his own strength. And as we submit ourselves to him, he directs all of our paths."

Pipeline to Hope

In a world filled with violence and hopelessness, we are called to be people of hope. But when we become one of the victims of the world's sickness, where do we go for that hope?

Madeline is a woman I met at a conference in North Carolina. After I did a teaching on hope, she stayed behind to share this story with me.

"After my first marriage ended in divorce, I decided I didn't want to marry again unless the man was totally family-centered, totally committed to my dauther Donna and me. When I met Ron, I just knew he was the one. He was so attentive and sweet. He wanted to join my church, and he was wonderful with Donna.

"About a year into the marriage, I began to suspect something was terribly wrong. Donna would run to me whimpering every time Ron came in the room. I won't even go into the details of how I discovered that he had been sexually abusing Donna.

"All that took place five years ago. We divorced immediately. Ron spent time in prison. I immediately relocated so Donna wouldn't have to grow up with the shame of the whole town knowing her story. She is still in therapy, and though she is doing very well, her therapist tells me she may struggle with this off and on all of her life. I have lived through hell—there's no other way to describe it. It has been the hardest thing I hope I ever have to go through.

"And yet in the midst of it all—the shock and grief and anger—I have never been without hope. The week before I found out about the abuse, the Lord gave me Psalm 71:5, and I didn't even know why. Then the day I found out about Ron, I went straight to my Bible where it was underlined, and I have clung to that verse like a life raft ever since. It says, "LORD, you are my hope." Not "you give me hope," but *"you are my hope."* That has been my reality.

"And, this, to me is one of the most incredible things he's brought out of all we've lived through. He's giving me a ministry to people with problems like mine. I've already counseled with several women who have gone through ordeals as bad or worse than mine, and I've been able to share my hope."

God longs for all of us to have the inner resource Madeline has had. When He pours his life into us, he is pouring out a hope that cannot be taken away.

Pipeline to Reconciliation

We live in a world where there is a tremendous distance between humankind and its Maker, tremendous hatred between nations and sexes and races and families. If there was ever a need for reconciliation, it is now. And this is the ministry we have been given in Christ.

My brother, Charlie, is an ordained Episcopal deacon, who holds monthly services at Angola Prison in Louisiana. I've never been inside a prison, but those who have tell me of the incredible darkness there. And yet Charlie tells a different story. He tells me, with light shining from his face, about the amazing revival going on in Angola; about the light of Christ moving powerfully among the prisoners; about the miracle of reconciliation drawing men together. Different denominations are worshiping together. Races that have hated and killed each other are finding a way to love. God is building bridges.

When Charlie preached recently at a Christian high school in Baton Rouge, he told one such story of reconciliation, the story of an inmate nicknamed Jet. Jet was born in Florida, the son of a white father and a Cherokee mother. Growing up between two worlds, he was accepted by neither.

When he was old enough, Jet left his family, joined a biker gang, and lived a life of recklessness, eventually killing a man in a barroom fight—a crime for which he was arrested and is now serving a life sentence.

Several years ago, Jet began coming to Charlie's services at Angola, at first hanging around on the fringes and gradually, over time, coming forward to talk to Charlie and others on the ministry team. Charlie could tell Jet was testing the team to see if they were "for real." He was also testing the gospel message to see if *it* was for real.

What Charlie didn't know at first was that Jet had been a member of the Aryan Nation, a white supremacist organization that flourishes in many prisons. Jet hated all other races, especially African-Americans. But the longer he was exposed to the love of Jesus, the more his heart began to change. One day he was invited by an African-American inmate named Archie to sit in as guitarist with a black gospel music group called Soul Purpose, and Jet soon became a regular member of the band.

Jet now describes Archie, the band leader, as a close friend and a "good dude." He marvels over the fact that during his Aryan Nation days he would have judged Archie by the color of his skin.

"These days," Charlie observes with a proud smile, "I call him 'St. Jet, the Evangelist,' since there's not a service goes by that he doesn't bring one or two new people with him—often they are black—to 'check us out.'" This January, Jet was baptized.

"Like all of our services," Charlie told me, beaming, "it was packed, and it was a glorious occasion indeed!"

The God who lived in Jesus the Son of God lives in Jet, the ex-biker turned evangelist. The God who was alive in Nazareth of Galilee is alive in Angola Prison of Louisiana, where he is turning despair into hope, hatred into love, and years of bitter separation between people and races into the reconciliation of the Father's heart. As Charlie puts it, "And they thought turning water into wine was something!"

A Pipeline to Joy

Living as a pipeline for God's living water is quite simply the secret joy of the Christian life. The more I read the Word, the more this amazing secret jumps out at me from verses I have known for years. It's as though God is peeling this revelation for me like an arti-choke till I am finally, gloriously getting to the heart of it!

When I give my testimony, I often share that I was besieged most of my younger life with what I termed "chronic restlessness." I was always convinced that, no matter what "party" I was attending, just down the street was a better party. I always felt that joy had just slipped out the door the minute before I arrived.

Now I realize that joy is understanding that Jesus lives his life in and through me. I'm excited about waking up in the morning because I know he is waiting to spend all day "doing my day" with me. I don't have to work up my own spiritual identity. I don't have to act a part or reinvent myself or make myself better or struggle with the shame of my old mistakes or have a foolproof plan for the rest of my life. I am free just to be who I am right now, today. These revelations have dissolved my restlessness. There is no better party down the street. This is the party! Christ in me and me in him. That's my joy, my freedom, my glory!

THE LAUGHTER OF GOD

When author Walter Lanyon's spirit grasped this reality, an incredible celebration was unleashed in him that changed his life, and he wrote these words:

> Deep in my soul I heard the Laughter of God, ringing in silvery cadences through the timbers of my being, breaking the human bonds and limitations as a strong yet gentle wind in the forest sweeps aside the strands of cobweb. The hard, fast knots that I had tied slipped loose, and the snarls of beliefs broke free. The

river of my human life, frozen by a thousand and one false ideas and teachings, broke joyously into expression and went bounding to the infinite sea of Life, to be lost and found at the same time. One dark cave of fear after another was illuminated by the light of this laughter, and swampy areas of sick thoughts were dried up instantly. Parched sands of hopelessness and futile efforts were drenched by the living waters, sucked in—absorbed instantly like a wave breaking on the sands. God laughing at me, and my puny efforts to make things happen; to make heaven appear; to attain the Sonship. Not the laugh of derision, but of infinite compassion, a laughter so deep and sweet, so pure and glorious that everything in the nature of struggle gave way before it.[2]

Wherever you are reading this book now, I want you to do something. Close your eyes. Open your heart, your hands, your spirit. Can you hear it? The deep, sweet laughter of God that is saying to you, "Come. Don't struggle any longer in your own strength. Let me give you my faith, my hope, my forgiveness, my spirit of reconciliation. Let me give you myself."

"I am the Root and the Offspring of David, and the bright Morning Star." The Spirit and the bride say, "Come!" And let him who hears say, "Come!" Whoever is thirsty, let him come; and whoever wishes, let him take the free gift of the water of life. (Rev. 22:16–17 NIV)

LET HIM LOVE THROUGH YOU: 1
THE OLD IS PASSED AWAY

*Read and reflect on these verses of Scripture
and the letter from your Abba that follows.*

But God's mercy is great, and he loved us very much. Though we were spiritually dead because of the things we did against God, he gave us new life with Christ. You have been saved by God's grace. And he raised us up with Christ and gave us a seat with him in the heavens. EPH. 2:4–6A

If anyone belongs to Christ, there is a new creation. The old things have gone; everything is made new! 2 COR. 5:17

My Dear Child,

Once you were dead. Your spirit was as parched and lifeless as a dry leaf swirling through an empty landscape. You went through the motions of life, but there was no life. You tried to gratify your desires in selfish ways, but you were unfulfilled. Then you turned to me, and the springtime of my mercy came breaking through the winter of your sinfulness. Now you are a new creation. Your old life is passed away. My Spirit has come alive in you. Stretched out ahead of you are unlimited horizons—gifts yet to be discovered, people yet to meet, challenges yet to overcome. No longer are you living merely to gratify your own needs, for your heart is my heart now. You are alive in my Son, and his love is flowing through you. There is new peace and hope and joy, free gifts of my grace. You are forgiven now. You are truly alive.

You are free!
Abba

WRITE A LETTER TO YOUR ABBA: 1

PRAYERS OF UNION

After reading and reflecting on God's words to you, write your own letter to him in your journal or in the space below, using the following guide:

1. In your letter to Abba God, reflect on what it means to be a new creation. Are there deeper dimensions of the "Christ-in-you" life that you would like to experience? Ask him to reveal to you more and more about this "union life"—you in him and him in you.

Dear Abba,

_____

_____

_____

_____

_____

_____

2. Now put down your pen. Ask Abba to speak to you. Sit quietly for ten minutes (or more) and listen to him in your heart. What is he saying to you about his indwelling Spirit? What personal words of love, guidance, or challenge do you hear? Write these out in your journal. (Remember, God's word in your heart will never conflict with his revealed Word in the Bible.)

CLOSING PRAYER: *Dear Abba, your love is a miracle! Old things have passed away, and you have made me a new creation. And now you—the God of the universe—have come to live in me. I welcome you, Lord! In Jesus' name, Amen.*

LET HIM LOVE THROUGH YOU: 2

GIVE UP YOUR LIFE

This is my command: Love each other as I have loved you. The greatest love a person can show is to die for his friends. You are my friends if you do what I command you. JOHN 15:12–14

Jesus said to all of them, "If people want to follow me, they must give up the things they want. They must be willing to give up their lives daily to follow me. Those who want to save their lives will give up true life. But those who give up their lives for me will have true life. LUKE 9:23–24

My Child,

What does it mean to die for your friends? Jesus went through the pain and shame and alienation of a public execution on the cross for you because you are his friend. He literally had nails hammered into his hands and feet, suffering terribly, and then he stopped breathing and physically died. Now he is asking you to love one another as he has loved you. Will this mean a physical crucifixion? Probably not. But it will mean giving your life as a vessel for him to live through as you follow him on his sacrificial, servant journey. Giving up your life isn't about being a weakling whose life is taken away. It's about being strong enough to surrender your life to be a pipeline for his power. There is no joy in the world like realizing that the incredible life and love and spirit power of Jesus is flowing freely through you. This is to be fully alive!

Yours for life!
Abba

WRITE A LETTER TO YOUR ABBA: 2
PRAYERS OF UNION

1. In your letter to Abba God, contrast the kind of death Jesus died to the kind of "death" we die in order to be "alive in Christ." Ask him any questions and express any feelings you have about this dying to live in him. Are you ready to live as a "pipeline" for his power?

Dear Abba,

_____

_____

_____

_____

_____

_____

_____

_____

2. Now put down your pen. Ask Abba to speak to you. Sit quietly for ten minutes (or more) and listen to him in your heart. What is he saying to you about being alive in Christ? What personal words of love, guidance, or challenge do you hear? Write these out in your journal. (Remember, God's word in your heart will never conflict with his revealed Word in the Bible.)

CLOSING PRAYER: *Dear Abba, I ask you to give me the courage to die to myself so that I can become a channel for your grace and a pipeline for your power. I can't live for you unless you live in me. Come, Holy Spirit. Fill and empower me. In Jesus' name, Amen.*

LET HIM LOVE THROUGH YOU: 3

I AM THE RIVER IN YOU

God is our protection and our strength.
He always helps in times of trouble.
So we will not be afraid even if the earth shakes,
or the mountains fall into the sea, . . .
There is a river that brings joy to the city of God,
the holy place where God Most High lives.
God is in that city, and so it will not be shaken. . . .
Nations tremble and kingdoms shake.
God shouts and the earth crumbles.
The LORD All-Powerful is with us;
the God of Jacob is our defender. PS. 46:1–2, 3–7

My Child,

Does the trouble around you seem insurmountable? Does it seem there is nowhere to turn? I am your strength, your hope, your power to overcome. Do not be afraid. However bad your personal circumstances seem today, steadfastly refuse to give in to fear. I am the peace, the hope, the love, the joy flowing through you. When the news media proclaim disaster, do not run scared with the world. Trust the One who lives in you and loves through you. See and believe in the Source of your power. There is a River whose streams flow with gladness into and through the hearts of my people. I am that River. I am your God. I am within you and will not fail you. Nations may rage, kingdoms may fall. But the sound of my voice breaks through earthly illusions.

I am the God who dwells within,
Abba

WRITE A LETTER TO YOUR ABBA: 3

PRAYERS OF UNION

1. Read again the first verses of Psalm 46 (shown on p. 202). In your letter to God the Father, thank him for the phrases that show his protection. Ask him what he is trying to reveal to you about the part of the psalm that describes him as the river bringing joy to the city. What does "the city" represent?

Dear Abba,

_____

_____

_____

_____

_____

_____

_____

2. Now put down your pen. Ask Abba to speak to you. Sit quietly for ten minutes (or more) and listen to him in your heart. What is he saying to you about allowing the River to flow through the city? What personal words of love, guidance, or challenge do you hear? Write these out in your journal. (Remember, God's word in your heart will never conflict with his revealed Word in the Bible.)

CLOSING PRAYER: *Dear Abba, thank you for pouring out the River of your Holy Spirit in me. Help me to trust the good news of your life in me more than I fear the rumblings of the bad news of the world. Continue to build me up in my inner being. I love you, Lord. Amen.*

LET HIM LOVE THROUGH YOU: 4

WALK AS A CHILD OF LIGHT

For you were once darkness, but now you are light in the Lord. Live as children of light (for the fruit of the light consists in all goodness, righteousness and truth) and find out what pleases the Lord. Have nothing to do with the fruitless deeds of darkness, but rather expose them. EPH. 5:8–10 NIV

That ye may be blameless and harmless, the sons of God, without rebuke, in the midst of a crooked and perverse nation, among whom ye shine as lights in the world. PHIL. 2:15 KJV

This is the message we have heard from him and declare to you: God is light; in him there is no darkness at all. If we claim to have fellowship with him yet walk in darkness, we lie and do not live by the truth. But if we walk in the light, as he is in the light, we have fellowship with one another, and the blood of Jesus, his Son, purifies us from all sin. 1 JOHN 1:5–7 NIV

Precious One,

You are my child—a child of the Light set down in a day of darkness. In this dark time, walk in faith knowing that I am the Light shining through you to others. Do not be afraid of this conspiracy of shadows. The fire of my Spirit burning in you can dispel all gloom. In me there is no shadow. In me there is no darkness at all. As my Light shines through you to others, they will be drawn to me. Keep the windows of your spirit clean so that my Spirit may shine brightly through your life to those trapped in the shadows and call them forth into my Light.

I am your,
Abba

WRITE A LETTER TO YOUR ABBA: 4
PRAYERS OF UNION

1. See your life as a lantern with no candle inside. The room is full of people huddled in darkness—children, old people, young couples. Few are speaking above a whisper. Now see the hand of your Abba placing the candle of his Spirit inside the lantern of your life and lighting it. See it spread light into every corner of the room. See the smiles of the people as they begin to talk to each other, to share their concerns, to become friends. In writing, tell Abba God how this picture relates to his life in you.

Dear Abba,

_____

_____

_____

_____

_____

2. Now put down your pen. Ask Abba to speak to you. Sit quietly for ten minutes (or more) and listen to him in your heart. What is he saying to you about being a child of light? What personal words of love, guidance, or challenge do you hear? Write these out in your journal. (Remember, God's word in your heart will never conflict with his revealed Word in the Bible.)

CLOSING PRAYER: *Dear Abba, I want to be a child of light. I desire to carry your love into the darkness of the world. Please light the candle of your Spirit in the lantern of my life. Amen.*

LET HIM LOVE THROUGH YOU: 5

I AM YOUR LIFE

I am the vine, and you are the branches. If any remain in me and I remain in them, they produce much fruit. But without me they can do nothing. JOHN 15:5

I was put to death on the cross with Christ, and I do not live anymore—it is Christ who lives in me. I still live in my body, but I live by faith in the Son of God who loved me and gave himself to save me. GAL. 2:20

God decided to let his people know this rich and glorious secret which he has for all people. This secret is Christ himself, who is in you. He is our only hope for glory. COL. 1:27

Dear Child of Mine,

This is my plan, my secret, my gift now unwrapped and open before you. My Son, Jesus Christ, in the power of his Holy Spirit, has come to save you from the futility of human striving. He will fill you with his own life, with the lifeblood of his Spirit flowing through you, as the sap of the vine flows through its branches. You will be free, and we will live in union, one with another. Through the Spirit in you, I will love and heal and help and forgive. I will do all the ordinary and impossible things that are part of life. This is reason for rejoicing!

Come be one with me,
Abba

WRITE A LETTER TO YOUR ABBA: 5

PRAYERS OF UNION

1. In writing, talk to God about Paul's "secret"—Christ in you. Why is it your only hope of glory? Ask the Lord to reveal more of this mystery to you.

Dear Abba,

_____

_____

_____

_____

_____

_____

_____

_____

_____

2. Now put down your pen. Ask Abba to speak to you. Sit quietly for ten minutes (or more) and listen to him in your heart. What is he saying to you about "Christ in you, the hope of glory" (Col. 1:27)? What personal words of love, guidance, or challenge do you hear? Write these out in your journal. (Remember, God's word in your heart will never conflict with his revealed Word in the Bible.)

CLOSING PRAYER: *Dear Abba, thank you that I don't have to understand everything totally before I can walk out my faith. Today I celebrate the amazing mystery of the fact that you dwell in me. I choose to die to myself and live by the power of your indwelling Spirit. This is my glory! Amen.*

TRUST HIM
IN THE FIGHT

TRUST HIM IN THE FIGHT

I love old movies set in the World War II era. One of my favorites is *Mrs. Minniver,* starring Greer Garson and Walter Pigeon. I guess one reason I'm partial to it is that it was released the year I was born. Mama always told me that her first outing after bringing me home from the hospital was a date with Daddy to see *Mrs. Minniver.* I can just picture Mama on her date dressed a little like Greer Garson herself with squared-off shoulder pads, a knee-length skirt, and chunky-heeled shoes.

But I mainly love the movie for its story. It is the tale of a family in England whose lives are changed by the war. The focus of the film is not what's happening on the front lines where Mr. Minniver and his son are fighting but what's happening on the home front where Mrs. Minniver and her daughter-in-law are fighting a battle of a different kind—a battle of food shortages, air raids, and basically trying to hold together a way of life whose very existence is being threatened. Mrs. Minniver is a wonderful heroine. She's an ordinary woman who is faced with danger she never expected, a woman who rises to the challenge for love of her family.

I saw *Mrs. Minniver* shortly after it came out on video, and I remember thanking God that we in the United States have never had to face a real war on our home soil. No sooner had I prayed that prayer than I heard him say silently but clearly, *You are in the midst of a deadly serious war that is being fought here on your home soil this very day, only you can't see it with your eyes. In this war you must look to me for the strength you will need to stand. You must know the dangers. And you must be familiar with the weapons I have put at your disposal.*

PAUL'S POWERFUL WARNING

The apostle Paul clearly warns us of this unseen battle in the sixth chapter of Ephesians:

> Finally, be strong in the Lord and in his great power. . . . Our fight is not against people on earth but against . . . the spiritual powers of evil in the heavenly world. That is why you need to put on God's full armor. Then on the day of evil you will be able to stand strong. And when you have finished the whole fight, you will still be standing. (vv. 10, 12–13)

The Message paraphrases Paul's warning like this: "This is no afternoon athletic contest that we'll walk away from and forget about in a couple of hours. This is for keeps, a life-or-death fight to the finish against the Devil and all his angels." There is a fresh urgency in these words. They say to us, "This is not a game! This is real! And the stakes are eternal!"

KNOW YOUR ENEMY

The Bible describes Satan, God's enemy in the battle, as the prince of darkness who masquerades as "an angel of light" (2 Cor. 11:14). He is pictured as a dragon, an ancient serpent who leads the whole world astray (see Rev. 12:9). He is called "the accuser" (Rev. 12:10) and Beelzebub, the prince of demons (Mark 3:22 NIV.) He is seen as "a roaring lion" seeking someone to devour (1 Pet. 5:8). It's not a pretty picture!

But, having said all that, I will add what my old friend Norman Grubb used to say to me whenever I would get shook up about the prospect of being "devoured" by the enemy.

"Yes," he would say with a smile, "he is a roaring lion. But he is a toothless, clawless lion. His teeth and claws were removed at Calvary!"

The point Norman was making is an important one to remember. Although we are in a battle, it is God's battle (see 1 Sam. 17:47), and we have nothing to fear, for we fight against a defeated foe. Jesus won the victory on the cross, and when we stand with him and in him, using his weapons, the victory is ours.

That is why we must learn to stand. We must go to spiritual boot camp and learn to handle God's weapons so that we can do our part.

THE FATHER'S PROVISION

The Father never leaves his children unprotected or ill-equipped. Everything we need to go through the unseen battle and remain standing is provided for us by our God. We are given both defensive and offensive equipment.

Defensive Equipment: Armor

The armor pictured in Ephesians 6 is modeled after that of a Roman soldier during the first century, when Paul was writing to the church at Ephesus.

1. The belt of truth. Paul's description of God's armor begins, "So stand strong, with the belt of truth tied around your waist" (Eph. 6:14a). Episcopal Bishop John Howe, in a teaching on spiritual warfare,[1] said that he had always wondered why Paul began listing the components of God's armor with the belt, which is found in the middle of the body, rather than starting at the top with the helmet. After studying and praying his way through Ephesians 6, he concluded that the order in which the armor is listed reveals the order of Satan's attack.

Satan always attacks God's children with falsehood and deception. He declares "good" what God has called bad or the other way around. If he can get us to doubt God, he's got us. In Eden he planted a seed of doubt in Eve by saying to her, "Did God really say . . . ?" (Gen. 3:1). If we are to stand against his subtle deception, we must have the belt of truth at the center of our being.

Jesus Christ is the Truth Incarnate. He dwells at the center of our being. The enemy's lies cannot shake our identity or our sense of worth, when we are covered by the belt of his truth, for we know who we are in him.

2. The breastplate of righteousness. We are next instructed to cover our hearts with the righteous character of Jesus Christ, "the breastplate of righteousness" (Eph. 6:14b NIV), for Satan's second line of attack is the heart, and his second choice of weapons is temptation. Notice that his enticement of Eve evolves from "Did God really say 'don't eat'?" to "Try it, you'll like it!" He holds out to her something so inviting and yet so harmless looking—a ripe, delicious piece of fruit. Now what possible harm could come from tasting an apple?

Like that innocuous-looking apple, many temptations look innocent in the beginning, and only later do they reveal their fangs. David and Karen Mains, in their children's fable, *Tales of the Kingdom,* paint an accurate portrait of the harm that can come from a harmless-looking temptation.

Princess Amanda, like all the other children in Great Park, knew that she was forbidden to keep dragon eggs, for though the eggs were beautiful, within six months they would hatch out and become full-grown dragons. Still, Amanda decided to disobey this rule and keep "just for a while" the two beautiful, amber-colored eggs she found. She hid them in her "Very Own Place" and forgot about them until one day a funny, awkward dragon hatchling pecked its way out of one of them, and Amanda fell in love with it.

She knew that she should take the hatchling to Caretaker, but she thought, *Perhaps I can tame it.* And as she fed and nurtured the hatchling, she found that she loved it more and more. What fun she had, teaching it things, playing with it, and watching it grow. Soon Amanda was spending so much time with her dragonet that she began to stay away from the Inmost Circle and even began to miss the Great Celebrations. As the beast began to come into its full growth, its hot breath began scorching the walls of Amanda's den, and when Amanda would ask it to do something, it began to defy her and do exactly as it wanted. It was only when the cruel and cunning full-grown dragon set Great Park on fire that Amanda finally saw what her disobedience had cost her and all of the residents of Great Park. Then she called on Caretaker, who gave her his hatchet to slay the dragon.[2]

I've often heard the saying, "sin fascinates, then it assassinates." It starts in a small way. We are initially drawn to it with the naive belief that we will be able to control it. But like Amanda's dragon, sin will turn on us. We cannot afford to entertain it even "just for a while," for our hearts are vulnerable. In order to stay pure in a generation rife with temptations, we need to keep our hearts covered with the righteous character of the Son of God.

3. The shoes of good news. Ephesians 6:15 tells us to wear on our feet "the Good News of peace to help [us] stand strong." When we think of shoes as they relate to battle, we might be inclined to think of marching, walking, or even running, but this verse does not refer to any of those three. It speaks instead of standing—standing strong in the gospel of peace.

Satan's third line of attack is aimed at throwing us off balance and causing us to fall. Never has the church been more in need of balanced, grounded Christians who know what they believe and what they are willing to stand for. On every front, the tenets and authority of moral, biblical Christianity are being undermined and attacked.

I am convinced that the following words from 2 Chronicles 20 are words for the embattled church of today. They are words that challenge believers to stand without fear for God's truth and allow him to handle the consequences.

"Don't be afraid or discouraged because of this large army. The battle is not your battle, it is God's. Tomorrow go down there and fight those people. . . . You won't need to fight in this battle. Just stand strong in your places, and you will see the LORD save you. (2 Chron. 20:15, 17)

4. The shield of faith. The next piece of armor, described in Ephesians 6:16, is "the shield of faith with which you can stop all the burning arrows of the Evil One." In the battles of ancient Rome, the tips of an enemy's arrows were sometimes dipped in poison and other times soaked in oil and set on fire. For this reason, the soldier needed overall protection. Any chink in his armor could cause his death. Huge rectangular shields the size of a door were therefore standard equipment for Roman soldiers. Holding his shield in front of him, a soldier could walk without fear of enemy arrows.

"But," you may protest, "I do not have a 'door-sized' faith!" That is no reason to stay out of the battle. Matthew 17:20 makes it clear to us that even faith as small as a mustard seed can accomplish tremendous things. But we must remember that faith in and of itself accomplishes nothing. It is faith in Jesus Christ that gives us power. He is our shield, and standing behind him—his might and his power—we will be protected from every onslaught.

5. The helmet of salvation. When Ephesians 6:17 instructs us to "Accept God's salvation as your helmet" it takes us to the ultimate battleground of the enemy, the mind. The enemy can win many a battle by filling our minds with depressing, discouraging, fearful, or confusing thoughts.

To put on the helmet of salvation is to cover our minds and our thoughts with the reality of our salvation. It is to say in the face of depression, "I belong to Jesus Christ. He is my savior and my strong tower—the lifter of my head and my confidence. I will not despair. He can work all things for good."

To put on the helmet of salvation is to say in the face of discouragement, "I will not receive discouragement. Jesus Christ has saved me for his own plans—plans to give me a future and a hope. He does not call me to do a task without supplying the power I will require. I will rely on his strength."

To put on the helmet of salvation is to say in the face of fear, "Jesus Christ loves me and his perfect love casts out all fear. He has not given me a spirit of fear but of love and of power and of a sound mind. I will trust the One who holds me in the hollow of his hand."

To put on the helmet of salvation is to say in the face of confusion, "I will look to Jesus, who is a God of order. I will trust him with all my heart and not depend on my own understanding. In quietness and confidence I will find my strength in him."

Wearing the helmet of salvation, we no longer entertain inner doubts or idle speculations. We no longer peer through the window of the world view, but we examine every thought and idea from the perspective of our salvation. "We demolish arguments and every pretension that sets itself up against the knowledge of God, and we take captive every thought to make it obedient to Christ" (2 Cor. 10:5 NIV).

Offensive Weapons

1. The chariot of prayer. "Pray in the Spirit at all times with all kinds of prayers, asking for everything you need. To do this you must always be ready and never give up. Always pray for all God's people" (Eph. 6:18). Prayer is our primary offensive weapon. It is like a chariot. In it, we can travel into battle. We can enter enemy territory and rescue captives. But Paul gives us two rules for driving this chariot:

- Always be ready. Have the wheels of your chariot oiled and in repair. Pray regularly and not just when an emergency arises.

- Never give up! Pray tenaciously. Don't just fling a prayer up to heaven like you might throw a penny in a well and then forget about it. Pray like the widow in Jesus' parable who pestered the judge until he gave her justice (see Luke 18:1–6).

Our son Andy wrote the following song, which encourages me to keep "flowing" in prayer, for my persistent, faithful prayers can literally carve away the mountains in my path:

A River Met a Mountain

A river met a mountain, there wasn't much to say.
The river said, "I'm flowing on," the mountain said, "I'm here
   to stay."
So the two collided in a clear, midsummer spray,
And the mountain thought the river was afraid.

The mountain told the river that he had to go around;
He said how things had always been, and nothing could
   change them now.

The river answered silently, as the mountain stood his ground;
The river kept on flowing slowly down.

[Chorus]
I want to flow, I want to flow,
I want to flow like a river through this life. [Repeat]

The mountain mocked the river as the two stood face to face,
But silently through centuries the river kept its pace
Till all unchangeability that he'd heard of was erased.
Where a mountain'd stood, a valley took its place.

('Cause) the river knew a simple truth that the mountain
    never heard;
He knew a river's journey's true if its Source is pure
And when the rain from Heaven comes, you can hear the river
    roar
And it can shake a mighty mountain to the core. . . .
    [Chorus]

(See) life is like a valley that we're all flowing through,
And there are many mountains here who say we can't intrude.
And if we believe their lies, I guess that makes them true,
But breaking through is what I choose to do,
Yes, breaking through is what I choose to do. . . . [Chorus]

A river met a mountain; there wasn't much to say.
The mountain was a fortress, but the water made a way.[3]

2. The sword of the Spirit. The next offensive weapon in our arsenal is "the sword of the Spirit, which is the word of God" (Eph. 6:17). A Roman soldier valued his sword above every other weapon. Without it he was lost.

We don't have much cause to use real swords in our modern world, but toy swords always played a big part in our sons' make-believe world when they were growing up. In their early years, Spike's woodworking shop turned out dozens of wooden swords on request for Curt, Andy, and all their friends. Later, when *Star Wars* was the big movie, all the neighborhood kids were saying, "the force be with you" and whacking it out with glow-in-the-dark, plastic, space swords.

But I saw a bit of toy weaponry recently that put me more in mind of "the sword of the Spirit" than any I've ever seen. Visiting with my friends Laura Barr and Joanne Hall in South Carolina one afternoon, we howled with laughter as we watched their sons David and Phillip wage war on each other with their new "Speak and Spray" plastic helmets. Each helmet came equipped with a voice-activated plastic hose, so each time one of the boys would yell at the other, the hose on his hat would spray his opponent with a hefty blast of water. Both boys ended up hoarse and totally drenched.

The "sword of the Spirit" is like the "Speak and Spray." It is word-activated. Each time the enemy comes against us, each time we are faced with one of his temptations, we slice down that temptation with the Word of God.

In the wilderness, Jesus was confronted with three temptations. In the face of every one of them, he spoke Scripture with strength and authority. He didn't "dialogue" with his enemy. He didn't argue or try to convince Satan. He used the Word of truth like a sword that cut down the tempting lie, stopping it in its tracks.

If we expect to win the war with God's words, we must be familiar with the Bible. We must read it often and prayerfully. If we will be faithful to do that, the Holy Spirit will be faithful to remind us of the verses we need just when we need them.

3. **The name of Jesus.** The name of Jesus is one of the most powerful weapons of our warfare. In the Book of Acts, people were saved, healed, and delivered in the name of Jesus (as they still are today!). Because the authorities recognized the power of Jesus' name, the disciples were jailed, flogged, and run out of town for using it. They were warned again and again not to preach or heal "in that name," but they continued to do so, because they knew they were dealing with the most powerful, life-changing name in the world. (See Acts 4:12.)

To pray in the name of Jesus is to pray in accordance with his will and in alignment with his character. It is to write a check that Jesus signs. And when that check is presented to the Father with the name of Jesus on it, the Father will cash it.

In the enduring hymn "A Mighty Fortress Is Our God," Martin Luther portrayed the power of the name of Jesus in counteracting the power of the enemy:

> The prince of darkness grim
> We tremble not for him
> His rage we can endure

For lo, his doom is sure:
One little word shall fell him.

The word that fells the enemy is the name of Jesus. In moments of darkness, it brings light. At times of despair, it brings hope. Into confusing circumstances, it brings order and peace.

Whenever I speak the name of Jesus I feel his presence enter my circumstances. I use his name in every kind of prayer from intercession to healing, from worship to warfare.

Often when I travel, I come into a hotel room in which I feel a spiritual heaviness. I have no way of knowing who has been in that room before me, and I know there is a strong possibility that I am sensing a dark spiritual presence. I have learned to pray the name of Jesus into the room as soon as I arrive. I proclaim him Lord of my life, Lord of the hotel room, of the hotel, the town, and the state. (Might as well cover all my bases while I'm at it!) It is amazing to feel the spiritual climate clear as his name is breathed into the atmosphere. There is power in his name!

4. The blood of Jesus. In spiritual warfare, there is no more powerful weapon than the blood of Jesus that was shed on Calvary's cross.

> You know that in the past you were living in a worthless way, a way passed down from the people who lived before you. But you were saved from that useless life. You were bought, not with something that ruins like gold or silver, but with the precious blood of Christ, who was like a pure and perfect lamb. (1 Pet. 1:18–19)

The reference to Christ as a "pure and perfect lamb" refers back to the twelfth chapter of Exodus, which describes the first Passover. God had warned Pharaoh to let the Israelites go or he would kill the firstborn in every Egyptian family. But Pharaoh refused. Thus God instructed the Israelites to kill a spotless lamb and mark the doorposts of their homes with its blood so that the angel of death, the destroyer, would pass over the homes of God's people, and they would be spared.

"Christ [is] our Passover lamb, [who] has been sacrificed" (1 Cor. 5:7). When praying for ourselves, for members of our family, or others in need, we can mark the doorposts of our homes and hearts with the blood of Christ so that our enemy, the destroyer, will pass over.

When my sons were teenagers and I was concerned about their lives—their friends, the choices they were making, the music they were listening to—I often marked the doorposts of their rooms when I prayed for them and asked the Lord to protect them by the blood of Jesus so that the destroyer would pass over and do them no harm.

5. The throne of praise. Though it may not seem very fierce or deadly, praise is a powerful weapon of spiritual warfare. We are told in Psalm 22:3 (KJV) that God himself inhabits the praises of his people, and the New Century translation of that verse declares, "You sit as the Holy One. The praises of Israel are your throne."

The enemy has no interest in hanging around where the Lord is reigning and in residence. To praise the Lord is to give him a palace to live in and a throne to reign on. And it is an invitation for the enemy to depart.

In the twentieth chapter of 2 Chronicles, praise is the weapon that routes the enemy. As Jehoshaphat prepares to go out into battle, he sends out singers ahead of his troops to praise the Lord. "As they began to sing and praise God, the LORD set ambushes for the people . . . who had come to attack Judah. And they were defeated" (2 Chron. 20:22). In fact, the enemy soldiers turned on each other and destroyed each other, which meant that Jehoshaphat's army never even had to fight.

Praise and worship can forestall many a battle for us, as they did for Jehoshaphat. We do well to stay in a place of praise.

6. Love: the ultimate weapon. Now we are clothed in spiritual armor and equipped with spiritual weapons, but we are not yet ready for the battle. The Lord would remind us that the most powerful weapon we can wield against evil is his love. We may not feel especially well equipped to do spiritual battle, but if we are lovers of God and lovers of others, that love will cover a multitude of shortcomings (see 1 Pet. 4:8). Love is the insignia that identifies us as his own (John 13:35), and it is the banner that flies over our battalion and our battlefield (see Song of Sol. 2:4).

To love others in a battle does not mean to compromise truth. We hate sin and deception because God hates it. But his Spirit in us allows us to hate sin while loving the sinner. It allows us to move to "the rhythm of relentless tenderness," the "heart music" of the One who loved us enough to die for us. It allows us to see that "in every encounter we give life or we drain it. There is no neutral exchange. We enhance human dignity or we diminish it. The success or failure of a given day is measured by the quality of our interest and compassion toward those around us."[4] We fight the enemy's weapons of hatred and indifference with the Lord's weapon of love.

A PERSONAL STORY

I learned about spiritual warfare the hard way—on the battlefield! In 1988 when our youngest son, Andy, was in high school, we began to notice a change in his behavior. His grades began to drop. His friend-ships began to change. His attitude toward us, which had always been loving, began to be cynical and rebellious.

We did what good Christian parents do. To begin with, we prayed. We talked to his teachers and his principal. And as his problems escalated, we got him tutors and took him to counselors. In fact, over a period of years, Andy saw three counselors, all of whom I pleaded with to help me identify the problem. Only the third was willing to help me label the black cloud that hung over our family. He suggested I attend a Twelve-Step meeting with a neighborhood friend, and as I sat in that meeting, I began to hear my feelings and experiences coming out of the mouths of other people. That was when I began to face the fact that I had been so afraid of: What we were dealing with was an alcohol and drug problem.

As Christians, when our problems get bigger, our prayer lives go deeper. As Spike and I shared our concerns with fellow believers, there were people all over the country praying for Andy. But no group was more faithful than the group of women who met at my friend Susan's house for prayer on Thursdays. They would arrive in their vans and station wagons, looking like ordinary wives and mothers with grocery lists, young children in tow, some of them dressed for tennis lessons. But when the door to Susan's house closed and they came into God's presence, they changed. Like Clark Kent becoming Superman in the phone booth, these women became prayer warriors!

Many days I was too wounded, broken, or burdened to pray myself. Then my sisters prayed for me. Though many of them did not even know Andy, week after week, they fought against the unseen powers of darkness that pulled my child toward destruction. They lifted him before the throne of God and asked for mercy. They also boosted my faith and helped me to stand in the battle.

Soon the clouds and confusion around me began to clear, and I could see that I was killing Andy with kindness—trying to be his Savior and his Holy Spirit. Trying to save him from any bad consequences for his behavior.

That was when the Lord gave us a new prayer: "Father," we would pray, "send some serious consequences for Andy's behavior that will create a crisis so he'll know he needs your help."

Within only a few months that prayer was answered. Andy was arrested, and during the night he spent in jail, he began to hear the still, small voice of God. That same week he was scheduled to begin a Christian mountain-climbing camp run by Summit Adventures in Bass Lake, California. Summit was life-changing for Andy. On a mountaintop overlooking God's spectacular creation, he gave his life to Jesus Christ. Later, at his own request, he entered a drug-rehab program and spent eight weeks "learning skills for living sober." Here is an excerpt from Andy's first letter to us from rehab that still brings tears to my eyes:

I think it says somewhere in the Bible that the Lord will make dry places fertile. This is what he is doing to me. I am only getting a glimpse of his plans for me through my newly opened eyes. I can laugh without stopping—smile and mean it. I feel great . . . Jesus—your name is like honey on my lips. Your spirit is like water to my soul, but most of all your word is becoming a lamp to my blistered and stumbling feet. I love you. This . . . has become my main prayer of thanks for light where there was darkness and hope where there was despair.

Seven years of sobriety have passed for Andy since that turn-around summer. He is married to a beautiful Christian woman named Jenni, and they had their first child—Kaylee Grace—in March of this year. Amazingly, God used Andy and Jenni for four years in youth ministry, working with many children of the same women who prayed for him in Susan's Thursday prayer group. That is God's awesome economy! The prayers of my friends for my child became bread upon the water that came back to bless their own children!

Now "we see through a glass, darkly" (1 Cor. 13:12 KJV). We don't understand exactly how or why our prayers work. We only know they do. And so we pray, gratefully and faithfully. When the Father calls us into battle, we follow Jesus, our captain, with total confidence, knowing that the victory is already ours!

TRUST HIM IN THE FIGHT: 1

I AM A GIANT SLAYER

*Read and reflect on these verses of Scripture
and the letter from your Abba that follows.*

David said to [the Philistine], "You come to me using a sword and two spears. But I come to you in the name of the LORD All-Powerful, the God of the armies of Israel! You have spoken against him. Today the LORD will hand you over to me, and . . . all the world will know there is a God in Israel! Everyone gathered here will know the LORD does not need swords or spears to save people. The battle belongs to him, and he will hand you over to us. . . . So David defeated the Philistine with only a sling and a stone." 1 SAM. 17:45–47, 50

Dear Child,

Do your problems loom above you like giants? Do they tower over your future and mock your confidence. Do not lose heart, for I am the God who slays giants. When your heart is right with me, I can overcome tremendous obstacles in and through you. Seek my will and my way, and I will fight your fight. I will equip you for the battle. A small stone hurled from a sling of faith can bring down a mighty opponent. What "giant" must you go out against today? Is it a financial problem? A difficult relationship? Is it a feeling of depression or anxiety about the future? Whatever it is, you can confront it with boldness today, for I will be with you. I possess power sufficient to overcome your enemies. Know me and trust me as David did, and today you can say with him, "The battle belongs to the Lord!"

*Victoriously,
Abba*

WRITE A LETTER TO YOUR ABBA: 1

PRAYERS OF SPIRITUAL WARFARE

*After reading and reflecting on God's words to you, write your own letter
to him in your journal or in the space below, using the following guide:*

1. In your letter, tell Abba God about the thing in your life that most
   makes you feel overwhelmed or powerless. Is it dealing with your
   spouse or your children? Is it the busyness of your life? Frustration on
   the job? Unrealistic expectations from others? Take your time describing your "giants" to God. Thank God for the story of David, and in the
   margin beside each of the "giants" you've listed, write "The battle is the
   Lord's!" or the initials "TBITL!"

   Dear Abba,

   _____

   _____

   _____

2. Now put down your pen. Ask Abba God to speak to you. Sit quietly for
   ten minutes (or more) and listen for him in your heart. What is he saying to you about his giant-slaying ability? What personal words of love,
   guidance, or challenge do you hear? Write these out in your journal.
   (Remember, God's word in your heart will never conflict with his
   revealed Word in the Bible.)

   CLOSING PRAYER: *Abba God, equip me to face my "giants" with a
   new kind of courage—a courage based on the knowledge that you are on
   my side and the battle is yours. Give me a picture of you as my ally and
   my constant companion as I go out against the giants in my life this day.
   Amen.*

TRUST HIM IN THE FIGHT: 2

BUILD YOUR HOUSE
ON THE ROCK

Jesus answered, "I am the way, and the truth, and the life. The only way to the Father is through me." JOHN 14:6

Enter through the narrow gate. The gate is wide and the road is wide that leads to hell, and many people enter through that gate. But the gate is small and the road is narrow that leads to true life. Only a few people find that road. MATT. 7:13–14

Everyone who hears my words and obeys them is like a wise man who built his house on rock. It rained hard, the floods came, and the winds blew and hit that house. But it did not fall, because it was built on rock. MATT. 7:24–25

Dear Child,

Some say, "It doesn't matter what you believe so long as you believe it sincerely." I say that it matters greatly, for you can be very sincerely wrong. Jesus is the way that leads to me; he is the truth that never fails; he is the life that is eternal. These are the realities on which you can stake your eternal soul. Don't be afraid of walking in the narrow way. You may not always be popular, but if you walk with me, you will never be alone. Don't be afraid of building your house on the rock of my word. The winds of life may rage and blow, but your house will stand though others fall. Don't be afraid to trust me in the midst of the battle, for I will give you the strength to stand up for what is right. Believe it!

Your Father and Friend,
Abba

WRITE A LETTER TO YOUR ABBA: 2
PRAYERS OF SPIRITUAL WARFARE

1. In your journal or in the space below, confess to Abba God any way you may have failed to stand for the truth. Write out a prayer asking him to help you walk in the narrow way, stand strong for his truth, and live without compromise.

   Dear Abba,

   _____

   _____

   _____

   _____

   _____

   _____

2. Now put down your pen. Ask Abba to speak to you. Sit quietly for ten minutes (or more) and listen to him in your heart. What is he saying to you about your integrity in the Christian life? What personal words of love, guidance, or challenge do you hear? Write these out in your journal. (Remember, God's word in your heart will never conflict with his revealed Word in the Bible.)

   CLOSING PRAYER: *Dear Abba, I confess to you that there have been times when I should have spoken your truth in a situation, yet I have been cowardly. Like Peter, I have denied you by my silence. Forgive me and strengthen me to be courageous in my stand for truth. I choose to follow you, knowing that you will equip me fully in every battle. And Abba, I ask you most of all to help me speak the truth in love. In Jesus' name, Amen.*

TRUST HIM IN THE FIGHT: 3

TALK BACK TO YOUR TEMPTATIONS

The devil came to Jesus . . . , saying, "If you are the Son of God, tell these rocks to become bread."

Jesus answered, "It is written . . . , 'A person does not live by eating only bread, but by everything God says.'"

Then the devil led Jesus to . . . a high place of the Temple . . . [and] said, "If you are the Son of God, jump down, because it is written . . . : 'He has put his angels in charge of you. . . .'"

Jesus answered him, "It also says in the Scriptures, 'Do not test the Lord your God.'"

Then the devil . . . showed [Jesus] all the kingdoms of the world. . . . [and] said, "If you will bow down and worship me, I will give you all these things."

Jesus said to the devil "Go away from me, Satan! It is written . . . , 'You must worship the Lord your God and serve only him.'" MATT. 4:3–10

My Dear Child,

The three temptations that came to Jesus in the wilderness will come to you, too. First, Jesus was tempted along the line of his appetite: "Turn this stone to bread." Satan knows your appetites well, and he will try to get you to choose them over my will. The second temptation came along the line of pride: "Throw yourself down from this temple and prove that you are God." Satan will always tempt you to walk the high road of pride rather than the low road of humble obedience. The third temptation came along the line of power: "I will give all this to you if you will worship me." Satan holds out an empty promise of power to those who will defect from my kingdom. All three temptations will try to pull you outside my will. Act as Jesus did. Speak my truth to each lie, and Satan will back off. Temptations are like explosives that can be dismantled by the truth of my Word.

Talk back to your temptations,
Abba

WRITE A LETTER TO YOUR ABBA: 3

PRAYERS OF SPIRITUAL WARFARE

1. In your journal or in the space below, write out any temptations that have come to you along the line of appetite, pride, or power. In your letter to Abba God, tell how you dealt with them and ask him for your wisdom in dealing with future temptations. Seek Scripture verses that "talk back" to each temptation you have listed and write them in your journal.

Dear Abba,

_____

_____

_____

_____

_____

_____

2. Now put down your pen. Ask Abba to speak to you. Sit quietly for ten minutes (or more) and listen to him in your heart. What is he saying to you about "dismantling" temptation? What personal words of love, guidance, or challenge do you hear? Write these out in your journal. (Remember, God's word in your heart will never conflict with his revealed Word in the Bible.)

CLOSING PRAYER: *Dear Abba, I know that I need to spend more time in your Word if I expect to use it as a weapon of warfare against the enemy's temptation. Send your Spirit to stir up in me a hunger for your truth. Sharpen my "sword" that I may use it more effectively. In Jesus' name, Amen.*

TRUST HIM IN THE FIGHT: 4

PRAY CONTINUALLY

Pray in the Spirit at all times with all kinds of prayers, asking for everything you need. To do this you must always be ready and never give up. Always pray for all God's people. EPH. 6:18

You know when I sit down and when I get up.
You know my thoughts before I think them. . . .
LORD, even before I say a word, you already know it.
Ps. 139:2, 4

Pray continually. 1 THESS. 5:17

Precious Child,

What do you think of prayer? Do you think of it as a duty to be accomplished? A responsibility to be carried out? A fringe activity you will get around to if you have the time? I am asking you to open yourself to a new understanding. Prayer is to the spirit what breathing is to the body. It is a natural and essential grace that feeds the spirit as oxygen feeds the body. When should you pray? At all times! Begin to think of prayer as a ceaseless flow of life in the hearts of those who love me. It is a moment-by-moment dialogue between Father and child. But it is so much more than forming ideas and sentences. Prayer is turning every thought to me. It is inviting me to be part of every idea and decision. I already know your unspoken thoughts, so direct those thoughts to me all day long, and you will be praying continually.

Lovingly,
Abba

WRITE A LETTER TO YOUR ABBA: 4
PRAYERS OF SPIRITUAL WARFARE

1. In your letter to your Abba God, reflect on how and why continual prayer acts as a weapon in spiritual warfare. In what ways can you begin to turn your thoughts to God throughout the day instead of only praying during set-aside times? Ask him to show you how.

Dear Abba,

_____

_____

_____

_____

_____

_____

_____

_____

2. Now put down your pen. Ask Abba to speak to you. Sit quietly for ten minutes (or more) and listen to him in your heart. What is he saying to you about continual prayer? What personal words of love, guidance, or challenge do you hear? Write these out in your journal. (Remember, God's word in your heart will never conflict with his revealed Word in the Bible.)

CLOSING PRAYER: *Dear Abba, send your Holy Spirit to strengthen my prayer life so that I may be a person of continual prayer. Beginning today, help me to turn toward you in every circumstance, bringing your light and your presence into each situation. In Jesus' name, Amen.*

TRUST HIM IN THE FIGHT: 5

GO OUT ARMED IN MY LOVE

The LORD says this to you: "Don't be afraid or discouraged because of this large army. The battle is not your battle, it is God's. . . . You won't need to fight in this battle. Just stand strong in your places, and you will see the LORD save you. Judah and Jerusalem, don't be afraid or discouraged, because the LORD is with you. . . ." 2 CHRON. 20:15, 17

Where God's love is, there is no fear, because God's perfect love drives out fear. 1 JOHN 4:18

Now we see a dim reflection, as if we were looking into a mirror, but then we shall see clearly. Now I know only a part, but then I will know fully, as God has known me. So these three things continue forever: faith, hope, and love. And the greatest of these is love. 1 COR. 13:12–13

My Child,

Fear can be the most paralyzing enemy of all. Hear the words that were prophesied to my people long years ago. "Don't be afraid or discouraged. . . . The battle is not your battle, it is God's." These are my words for you today. I know how difficult it can be to stand for me in a world that is increasingly hostile to me and my Truth. But you don't need to go out with your boxing gloves on, viewing every person as an opponent. Go out armed in my love instead and stand for me. Go out to a world of hurting people and love them for me. And when there are battles to fight, I will fight them for you. Your insight is limited now. But know this: There is no need to live in fear, for my love overcomes fear. In this battle against evil, my love is the most enduring and powerful weapon of all.

Go out in love,
Abba

WRITE A LETTER TO YOUR ABBA: 5
PRAYERS OF SPIRITUAL WARFARE

1. In your letter to Abba God, tell him of one or more times fear has held you back on your spiritual journey. Reflect on fear and love as opposites. Has love ever overcome fear in you? Ask the Lord to make you less fearful and more loving.

Dear Abba,

---

2. Now put down your pen. Ask Abba to speak to you. Sit quietly for ten minutes (or more) and listen to him in your heart. What is he saying to you about love overcoming fear? What personal words of love, guidance, or challenge do you hear? Write these out in your journal. (Remember, God's word in your heart will never conflict with his revealed Word in the Bible.)

CLOSING PRAYER: *Dear Abba, thank you for your promise that you will fight the battle for us. I choose to give you my fear and to "go out" armed in your love today. Be both strong and compassionate in me. Help me to hate sin but love the sinner. Help me to walk where your Son walked, bringing his Spirit to a world that needs him so badly. Amen.*

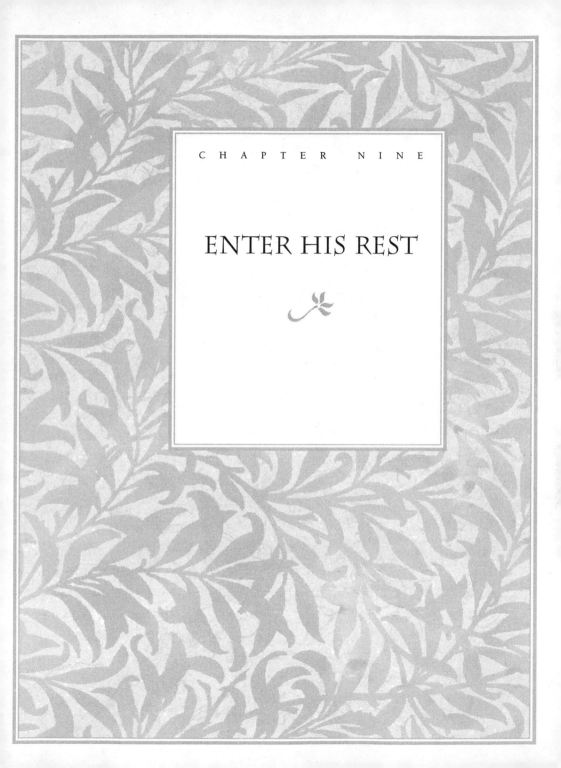

C H A P T E R   N I N E

ENTER HIS REST

ENTER HIS REST

Five years ago Spike and I did something most of our friends considered somewhere between eccentric and insane. We sold the large, comfortable house where we had raised our children in a town we had called home for twenty years, and we moved full time into our tiny weekend cabin in the country. We moved from a busy life in a busy city of 350,000 people to the snail's-pace existence of a community of 350 people.

The downtown area of our new hometown consists of a small mom-and-pop grocery store-filling station, Mitchell's Mercantile, a hardware store, and a recently added video store. Most of the time, Mitchell's has a couple of signs out front—one reading "hunting licenses" and one reading "Crickets and Worms" since hunting and fishing are the main extracurricular pastimes of the local folk.

I'll never forget our first visit from my sister, who lives in Washington, D.C. She scoped out our new locale and said somewhat facetiously, "What? No cappuccino in the whole town?"

"Oh," I assured her, "it's only a matter of time before Mitchell's gets a cappuccino machine. Only then they'll have to change their sign to read 'Crickets, Worms, and Cappuccino.'"

That hasn't happened yet.

RESTING LESSONS

I must admit the site of our cabin is very beautiful and restful. We are situated on a forty-foot bluff looking down on a deep, clear, slow-moving, sand-bottomed Alabama river. We are surrounded by peace and quiet on all sides.

In fact, we are surrounded by so much peace and quiet that I almost went crazy the first two years we lived here. I was like a baby having a tantrum. I couldn't seem to get the rush and hurry out of my system.

My withdrawal was slow and painful. But the Lord held me close to him until my tantrum was over, and when I became quiet, I was able to see the gift he was trying to give me. He was trying to teach me to rest.

It seems absurd to think that a person should need resting lessons. Surely rest is something that should come naturally. It was part of God's original plan for his creation. In fact one-seventh of every week was supposed to be set aside for it. But many of us modern types have managed to trim that percentage to virtually zero.

Rest is neither valued nor rewarded in our culture. In fact in some circles it is seen as synonymous with sloth. Corporate America considers "downtime" a rousing game of handball or tennis, a challenging workout, or a three-mile power walk. These things are wonderful for upping the heart rate, but they have nothing to do with rest. And they have even less to do with "the prayer of rest."

A MODERN-DAY TRAGEDY

Though we are people who have an innate need for rest, we live in the midst of a generation that knows very little about it. This was made clear to me recently as I did a little inadvertent eavesdropping.

I was shopping for a birthday gift for my mom. Since her birthday is December 4, the department store I was in was already beautifully decorated for Christmas and crowded with shoppers. At the cosmetics counter, I overheard the conversation of two beautifully dressed women whose words hit me like dialogue from a modern-day tragedy.

"I'm really an unhappy person, Marcy," one of them was saying to the other. "I can't pretend I'm not. All I do is work and sleep. My life has gotten away from me. I can't slow it down."

The tragic part of what I heard that day was that the woman speaking felt so out of control. She claimed to want a less hectic pace, but she saw herself as inescapably trapped.

There is a way out. It has been provided for us by the God who knows our need for rest—the God who put that need in us. We are given the promise in Hebrews 4:10 that "anyone who enters God's rest will rest from his work as God did." But the fact that resting is not always an easy choice is made evident by verse 11, which encourages us to "try as hard as we can to enter God's rest so that no one will fail by following the example of those who refused to obey."

What is the rest we are called "to obey," and how can it make a difference in lives that are restless, overcommitted, and chaotic?

The Eye of the Hurricane

"Through the Prayer of Rest, God places his children in the eye of the storm. When all around us is chaos and confusion, deep within we know stability and serenity. In the midst of intense personal struggle, we are still and relaxed. While a thousand frustrations seek to distract us, we remain focused and attentive. This is the fruit of the Prayer of Rest."[1]

Seeing the prayer of rest as "the eye of the storm" is a concept I can relate to. Spike and I were both born and have lived all our lives in "hurricane country." Our move from Louisiana to Alabama twenty-five years ago took us from one hurricane-prone location to another. I've probably gone through a dozen or more of these giant, erratic storms in my lifetime, but never have I experienced anything quite like the hurricane season of 1994, when two different hurricanes (Erin and Opal) headed directly for our front yard, one right after the other!

Erin is the one I will never forget. Though I have been in stronger winds, I have never been more terrified. What made Erin particularly fearsome was the fact that it was a daytime storm, and so not only were we hearing the deafening howl of the winds, we were also seeing its effects as, with each incredible gust, branches were snapped off and hurled through the sky like airborne weapons and huge trees around our cabin bent down to the ground, begging the winds for mercy.

Then, over our house came the eye of the storm, the quiet center of the circular weather system, like a hole in the doughnut of a disaster. It was amazing. One minute the cabin was shuddering in the shrieking winds, and the next minute the air became unbelievably still and quiet.

We walked outside for a few brief moments and surveyed the destruction. Several trees were down, including our largest oak, which had snapped off and lay like a dead body on the ground. But we didn't stay outside for long, for we know hurricanes, and we knew that just the other side of the eye was more wind, rain, and devastation.

Like the eye of the storm, the prayer of rest is a place of serenity in the midst of turmoil. Though we cannot control the chaotic world around us, we can, by choosing to rest in God's presence, stay in the quiet center of the storm while the world whirls on at its own frenzied fury.

A SILENT RETREAT

My first experience with the prayer of rest revealed not only my deep need for it but my total lack of understanding as to how it works. The setting was a beautiful, old, stone Roman Catholic monastery tucked away behind a high wall in downtown Mobile. Entering those walls is like going back in time. Huge, moss-draped oaks blanket the grounds in shade, and a sanctuary of quiet lies behind massive oak doors.

I had been invited by a friend to take part in an annual silent retreat for women, and since I was the mother of two very noisy, active little boys, the prospect sounded positively delightful. No sooner had Spike agreed to keep Curt and Andy than my bags were packed! But as excited as I was, I must admit, I was a little doubtful as to whether I would actually be able to keep my mouth shut.

About twenty-five women began arriving around 4 P.M. After a short time of meeting and greeting, we were given the retreat schedule and assigned rooms on the second floor. I walked noiselessly down the long corridor in my "quiet-soled" shoes and located my room.

It was a cubbyhole of a space, a cell really, about eight-by-eight, containing a single bed, a tiny wardrobe, and a desk. I loved it! In it, I was not responsible for a whole household. I was only me. I felt like a little girl in my Daddy's house. I looked at my watch. An hour and fifteen minutes 'til dinner.

Perfect, I thought. Just a little time to unpack my stuff and start being still. Wrong. Being still, I discovered, was not a concept in my body's vocabulary.

During those two days of quiet, we were being taught by our retreat leader how to enter the prayer of rest. And as we were being given the opportunity to practice what he was preaching, I found out how many ways the mind can sabotage the spirit when it comes to resting. These were among the things that rose up against my rest during those quiet hours:

1. I found myself wondering what was happening at home. Would Spike remember to take Andy to the birthday party?

2. I found myself thinking about everything I had to do next week. This was a perfect time to make a list.

3. I thought of all the letters I owed to people. No sense wasting this time. I could just jot down a few quick notes.

4. I thought about that good book I had chanced to stick in my backpack. What would one chapter hurt?

5. I thought about . . . *zzzzzzzzzzz*. That's right. Smack dab in the middle of communing with God. The big snooze.

6. But hardest of all to fight, in the midst of the quiet, was my urge to work. A lyric idea would float up to the surface of my mind. *After all,* I'd reason, *this is a song about rest. Think how many people it could help.* (Oh, how much easier it is for me to *write* about rest than it is to rest!)

Unheard Music in the Quiet

It is always difficult in the beginning to stop striving, to unplug all of those insistent little messages from our minds, to trust the quiet and the inactivity. But if we will enter God's rest, truly seeking him, we will discover that often God's gifts are hidden more in what we don't do than in what we do. And we will find that there is unheard music in the quiet, unseen dancing in the stillness, and the glorious hand of Creativity at work in our inactivity.

Frederick Buechner, in his book *The Hungering Dark*, describes the way he experienced one of his most meaningful teaching times, quite by chance, on a day when he didn't teach a thing. Walking to his classroom one winter afternoon, he noticed the beginnings of a beautiful sunset. When he got to the classroom, the lights were all on and his students were "chattering" noisily, as usual. On impulse, Buechner flicked off the lights. The following is his description of what happened next:

> The room faced west so as soon as it went dark, everything disappeared except what we could see through the windows, and there it was—the entire sky on fire by then, like the end of the world or the beginning of the world. You might think that somebody would have said something . . . and you might have expected a wisecrack or two . . . but the astonishing thing was that the silence was as complete as you can get it in a room full of people, and we all sat there unmoving for as long as it took the extraordinary spectacle to fade slowly away. For over twenty minutes nobody said a word. Nobody did anything.
>
> We just sat there in the near-dark and watched one day of our lives come to an end. . . . [and] in a way the sunset was the least of it. What was great was the unbusy-ness of it. It was taking unlabeled, unallotted time just to look with maybe more than our eyes at what was wonderfully there to be looked at without any obligation to think any constructive thoughts about it or turn it to any useful purpose later.[2]

Entering God's rest is very like what happened in Buechner's classroom. Without any agenda, we come to God. We intentionally let go of our own efforts to pull his strings, and we surrender to his purposes. We turn out the lights of our own self-effort and allow ourselves to be overwhelmed by the flame of his amazing love.

EXPECTING NOTHING AND
EXPECTING EVERYTHING

Recently our artist-friend Marilyn Stewart learned a powerful lesson about turning out the lights of her self-effort. In April 1995, Marilyn had heard the Lord tell her to draw him. For one and a half years, she attempted sculpting, painting, and drawing the face and/or the form of Jesus Christ but felt that each attempt fell short of her image of who he really is.

Finally, in September of 1996, the Lord told Marilyn to stop striving and trust him. She closed her eyes, and in prayer she saw her Lord kneeling in the Garden. With her eyes still closed, she drew him as he appeared. When she opened her eyes she saw an image so moving, so filled with life, it brings tears to the eyes of those who see it. In it you can almost see, by the elongation of the hands and fingers, the Lord lifting his hands in agony to the Father.

Marilyn often draws the Lord while she is in prayer now. Before drawing, she asks the Lord to give her a picture of himself. Then she draws what she "sees" within. What she sees is the real, living Christ, sometimes talking or moving. In drawing the crucifixion, the pain Marilyn saw was almost unbearable. She could see the tears dripping off of his cheeks.

Unlike any of her work in any other medium, Marilyn's line drawings of the Lord are like prayers of rest. She comes to the Lord with no agenda—expecting nothing and expecting everything. Her spirit is quiet and open to whatever he will place in her heart. And as she draws, he reveals himself to her as the One who lives within.

INGREDIENTS OF THE PRAYER OF REST

Maybe by now you're wanting to say to me, "Okay, Claire. Stop with the metaphors already! Just say what you mean!" Being a lyricist, my mind is constantly caught in metaphors and similes. It's an occupational hazard. I have told you that the prayer of rest is like being in the eye of a hurricane. I have told you that it is like watching a magnificent sunset in an evening sky. I have told you that it is like drawing Jesus with your eyes closed. Perhaps now you are ready for me to say something a little more practical. Here then, in the plainest terms I know, are some steps to take in entering his rest.

Seek Solitude and Silence

The prayer of rest begins as we come very quietly to the Lord in solitude. I realize solitude is difficult to come by in some households, but as I have encouraged you in other chapters of this book, put a high priority on finding a place apart where you can bring your heart before the Lord. It can be a broom closet or a bathroom or a basement.

Jesus was surrounded by people all the time. When he wasn't teaching and healing huge crowds, he was walking along the road instructing his disciples in the ways of the kingdom. Jesus had no private room of his own, no way to shut out the world. But he knew the value of solitude and the necessity of time alone with his Father, so he rose early and walked the hills in his Father's presence. If Jesus needed solitude and silence, how much more do we!

Trust Totally

We must enter God's rest with a complete dependence on him, a willingness to be out of control, a total trust. This means not trying to manipulate the outcome of our prayer time. The outcome is up to God.

What a blessing to let go of our cares knowing that he holds them in his hands. What a blessing to rest in his presence, knowing that he never does. ("He who guards you never sleeps. He who guards Israel never rests or sleeps. . . ." Ps. 121:3–4.)

My friend Micki Ann Harris echoed those sentiments from Psalm 121 when she wrote, "While you are resting, Your Heavenly Father will continue counting the hairs on your head, rotating the earth, clothing the lilies, keeping hearts beating and lungs filled with air. While you are resting, He will continue to fight your unseen battles and answer prayers. He will continue to create ideas you never could have imagined and solutions you wouldn't have dreamed of."[3] This is the precious place of rest in our God.

Focus Your Heart

The position of the body in the prayer of rest is not so important as the condition of the heart, but finding a comfortable place to sit helps us maintain an open and attentive heart attitude. Though the prayer of rest involves quietly waiting, it is not a totally passive spiritual stance. We wait expectantly aware of his presence, with our hearts focused and our minds inwardly set on him. And should the mind begin to stray, we quietly take it by the hand as we would a small child and lead it back into the presence of the Lord.

Take Your Time

In experimenting with any new endeavor, most of us want a rule book, but the prayer of rest resists rules. It is by nature a prayer of freedom.

How long is long enough? Fifteen to twenty minutes in the morning can make a tremendous difference in your day. An hour could be better. And some proponents of the prayer of rest suggest taking day-long or weekend retreats for quiet.

Spike often plans a totally quiet, unstructured day or two in which he communes with God in everything he does. Here is a poem he wrote at the beginning of one such retreat in 1985:

Morning Song
Today I would have a gentle day.
Seamless slow would be its pace,
yet focused
Upon what Creation has to teach.
Hand bent to earth and flower,
eye to flower and bird,
ear to bird and brook.
Heart to God.

And tomorrow?
Another yet the same.[4]

Just "Be"

We come to the prayer of rest knowing where God can be found. He is within. In our prayer-team meetings at church, we are taught to remind ourselves often that "Another dwells in me—Jesus Christ dwells in me." When we come silently, focusing our hearts upon the Lord, we are giving ourselves permission to rest completely in that reality.

We are not to think of our sins or confess them. We are not even necessarily to worship God, though a state of worship may come over us as we are in his presence. This is simply a time of being with him. As two newlyweds in love might spend time together just looking at each other or lying quietly in each other's arms, we dwell quietly in the presence of the Beloved, our God and our Resting Place.

Don't Analyze the Results

One temptation after enjoying the prayer of rest is to grade ourselves. *How did I do?* says our cognitive self. *What was accomplished?* But in the prayer of rest it is better to leave the results to God. He knows what he is working on as we bring ourselves into his presence. We may feel that nothing worthwhile has happened. But we can be confident that God is at work.

My brother Charlie, who relies strongly on times of contemplative, resting prayer, contends that though he doesn't understand how it works, spending quiet time with God every morning "puts fuel in [his] furnace that stays lit all day." Being still in God's presence provides the energy he needs to function in a demanding job, a full family life, and a busy ministry. For Charlie, the prayer of rest and the active life are simply two sides of the same coin. He carries the rest he finds alone with God each day "out into the world, into its turmoil and its fitfulness."[5]

A SUMMER MEMORY

The Father's still, small voice is calling each of us to let go of the world's tensions and come into his rest.

One of the most restful places in the world for me as a child was riding in the car when my dad was driving. I have vivid early-childhood memories of traveling through some dark summer night on a family vacation with the windows rolled down and the warm summer breeze blowing over us. There we would be on some road we had never traveled, in some state we had never known, headed for some city we had only seen on a map. Nothing was familiar or customary or usual, and yet I had not a care in the world. On those nights I would slip into the sweetest, deepest, safest-feeling sleep simply because I knew my dad was behind the wheel. I didn't need to know how far he planned to travel or what hotel he planned to stop at. I was content to rest in the fact that he was in control.

The prayer of rest is like that. It is setting aside the cares and the tensions of our lives and allowing our Abba God to "plan the trip." It is feeling the wind of the Holy Spirit through the open windows of our souls. It is settling down in God's presence and learning how to trust.

When I finally stopped having my temper tantrum after our move to the country, I asked the Lord to lead me to passages in his Word that would explain our new life as he wanted it to be. One of the very first verses he lead me to said this:

> Come to me, all of you who are tired and have heavy loads, and
> I will give you rest. (Matt. 11:28)

This verse is for each of us. You don't have to move into a log cabin in the country or go on a silent retreat to enter his rest. My prayer is that you will find a spiritual retreat in the very midst of your heart right where you are today.

ENTER HIS REST: 1
I WILL GIVE YOU REST

*Read and reflect on these verses of Scripture
and the letter from your Abba that follows.*

Come to me, all of you who are tired and have heavy loads, and I will give you rest. Accept my teachings and learn from me, because I am gentle and humble in spirit, and you will find rest for your lives. The teaching that I ask you to accept is easy; the load I give you to carry is light. MATT. 11:28–30

My Child,

Though you may hide your weariness from others, you cannot hide it from me. I see it in your eyes and in your spirit. You are tired of waking up each day facing the same problems and feeling that there is no one who really understands. You are tired of trying to hold things together in your own strength. Tired of the things that drain you of your energy and leave you depleted—trying relationships, financial problems, daily decisions. You long to lean back and rest the full weight of your burdens on Someone who is big enough to hold them up. Oh my child, I have waited for this weariness in you so that you would finally learn to let go and let me be God. Look at my Son. Learn from him. He didn't try to be strong in his own strength. He was humble enough to look to me. If he could live his human life like that, don't you think you should try it? Come to me. Hand me those heavy weights. Let me give you my rest.

I love you,
Abba

WRITE A LETTER TO YOUR ABBA: 1
PRAYERS OF SERENITY

After reading and reflecting on God's words to you,
write your own letter to him, using the following guide:

1. In your journal or in the space below, tell Abba God what things "drain your energy." Now come to him as he is inviting you to. Tell him that you want his rest and invite him to take your stress.

   Dear Abba,

   _____

   _____

   _____

   _____

   _____

2. Now put down your pen. Ask Abba to speak to you. Sit quietly for ten minutes (or more) and listen to him in your heart. What is he saying to you about giving you his rest? What personal words of love, guidance, or challenge do you hear? Write these out in your journal. (Remember, God's word in your heart will never conflict with his revealed Word in the Bible.)

   CLOSING PRAYER: *Dear Abba, thank you for being there for me to lean back on. Thank you for seeing the weariness in me even when I don't see it in myself. Help me to trust you more and worry less. I need your rest to flood my body and my spirit. Come, Holy Spirit and refresh me now. Amen.*

ENTER HIS REST: 2
YOU MUST LEARN
TO BE STILL

Then a great and powerful wind tore the mountains apart . . . , but the LORD was not in the wind. After the wind there was an earthquake, but the LORD was not in the earthquake. After the earthquake came a fire, but the LORD was not in the fire. And after the fire came a gentle whisper. . . . Then a voice said to him, "What are you doing here, Elijah?" 1 KINGS 19:11–13 NIV

My Child,

Your problem is not that you don't know how to pray. It is that you don't know how to sit still! If you truly want a relationship with me, you must stop compulsively rushing around. You must turn off the noise in your frantic, frenetic world and come in quietness to me. Listen for my gentle voice within you. I don't roar like a freight train or shriek like the wind. I whisper the intimate words of a Friend. Come to me; enter my rest; hear my whispered words in the chamber of your spirit. I am ever speaking, ever waiting for you to hear me.

With a deep love for you,
Abba

WRITE A LETTER TO YOUR ABBA: 2
PRAYERS OF SERENITY

1. In your letter to Abba God, express any frustrations you may have about being "too busy for your own good." Tell him why you think you have a problem with it. Ask him to teach you the rhythms of his rest.

   Dear Abba,

   _____

   _____

   _____

   _____

   _____

   _____

   _____

   _____

2. Now put down your pen. Ask Abba to speak to you. Sit quietly for ten minutes (or more) and listen to him in your heart. What is he saying to you about being still in his presence? What personal words of love, guidance, or challenge do you hear? Write these out in your journal. (Remember, God's word in your heart will never conflict with his revealed Word in the Bible.)

   CLOSING PRAYER: *Dear Abba, I am constantly complaining about my busyness, but I don't seem to be able or willing to change myself. Lord, help me to yearn for stillness more so that I can concentrate on you. Teach me how to enter your rest. In Jesus' name, Amen.*

ENTER HIS REST: 3
COME AWAY WITH ME

And when you pray, do not be like the hypocrites, for they love to pray standing in the synagogues and on the street corners to be seen by men. I tell you the truth, they have received their reward in full. But when you pray, go into your room, close the door and pray to your Father, who is unseen. Then your Father, who sees what is done in secret, will reward you. MATT. 6:5–6 NIV

[Jesus] went up on a mountainside by himself to pray. When evening came, he was there alone. MATT. 14:23 NIV

My Child,

When the world and its chaos closes in on you, do as Jesus did: Run to me in prayer. For only in the solitary world of prayer can you be equipped to live in the crowded world of others. In the solitude I will siphon off the poisons of resentment and jealousy, covetousness and fear. In the solitude I will fuel you with my mercy and gentleness, my patience and grace. And as you return day after day to the peace and solitude of prayer, you will begin to find yourself more and more able to carry that peace and solitude away with you, back into the noisy, crowded world, like a turtle carries its home upon its back.

Come away with me,
Abba

WRITE A LETTER TO YOUR ABBA: 3

PRAYERS OF SERENITY

1. In your letter to Abba God, describe to him your need for his serenity and rest in the midst of a busy life. Ask him to encircle you with his shell of quietness and gentleness into which you can retreat when you need to be with him.

Dear Abba,

_____

_____

_____

_____

_____

_____

2. Now put down your pen. Ask Abba God to speak to you. Sit quietly for ten minutes (or more) and listen for him in your heart. What is he saying to you today about your need for stillness and peace? What personal words of love, guidance, or challenge do you hear? Write out in your journal any words, phrases, or sentences he speaks to you. (Remember, God's word in your heart will never contradict his revealed Word in the Bible.)

CLOSING PRAYER: *Dear Abba, you know my need for a refuge where I can run to you when my life is overwhelming. But even without a physical "place" to go to, I can begin to quiet myself. Help me to live within your quietness today. Help me to hear your still, small voice. Amen.*

ENTER HIS REST: 4

BE TRANSFORMED
IN MY PRESENCE

Do not conform any longer to the pattern of this world, but be transformed by the renewing of your mind. ROM. 12:2A NIV

In thy presence is fulness of joy;
    at thy right hand there are pleasures for evermore.
    PS. 16:11 KJV

My Dear Child,

You can only hope to escape being molded into the world's image by withdrawing from the world for regular, quiet, concentrated times of refreshment in my renewing presence. Here you can drop the weight of your compulsions and quiet the inner muttering of your mind. Here you can put down your narrow agenda and let me show you the wide vistas of my perfect plan for you. Here your true self, which has been caged with the wild animals of your worries, can be released to dance in the light and freedom of my love. In my presence there is fullness of joy and pleasures that have no expiration date! Come into my presence, my child. Let my love reshape you.

Your loving Abba,
God

WRITE A LETTER TO YOUR ABBA: 4
PRAYERS OF SERENITY

1. In your letter to Abba God, tell him what "tools of the world" have molded your thinking. Television? Social pressures? Others? Reflect on the effect these things have had on you. Give him permission to remold you as you turn more and more of your life over to him.

Dear Abba,

_____

_____

_____

_____

_____

_____

_____

_____

2. Now put down your pen. Ask Abba God to speak to you. Sit quietly for ten minutes (or more) and listen for him in your heart. What is he saying to you today about being shaped by his love? What personal words of love, guidance, or challenge do you hear? Write out in your journal any words, phrases, or sentences he speaks to you. (Remember, God's word in your heart will never contradict his revealed Word in the Bible.)

CLOSING PRAYER: *Dear Abba, I come today asking you to shape my life. I don't want it to take the shape of this sometimes-twisted world. I want to be formed instead by your perfect love into the image of Jesus. As I come into your presence I give you permission to remold me. Amen.*

ENTER HIS REST: 5

I WILL REST IN YOU

Now, since God has left us the promise that we may enter his rest, let us be very careful so none of you will fail to enter. Heb. 4:1

Love is not happy with evil but is happy with the truth. . . . It always trusts, always hopes, and always remains strong. 1 Cor. 13:6–7

You should be a light for other people. Live so that they will see the good things you do and will praise your Father in heaven. Matt. 5:16

My Child,

What am I calling you to this day? I am calling you to a life of rest in me. Far from being passive, my rest at the center of you becomes the wellspring of all your actions. Out of my rest will flow many acts by which you will be known as my child. You will love me and love others. You will resist worry and fear, looking to the future with hope. You will let my light shine through you to those in darkness. You will make your home a place of welcome and your heart a fountain of encouragement. You will turn from the enemy's lies and resist his condemnation. You will saturate yourself with my truth and believe in my love for you. You will wear my mercy like a crown and my righteousness like a cloak about your shoulders, for you are my child and I am your Father.

Rest in me,
Abba

WRITE A LETTER TO YOUR ABBA: 5
PRAYERS OF SERENITY

1. See yourself in God's presence. See him digging a well in the center of your being, removing from you all anxiety, stress, or ungodly ambition that motivate your actions. In your letter to Abba God, describe what you see him digging out of you. Name each one, confess it as sin and give it to him. Now invite him to pour his love and his rest into that well. As his rest is poured out, see it become a fountain, full of energy and life in you. Write about what kind of life will spring out of that fountain.

Dear Abba,

_____

_____

_____

_____

_____

2. Now put down your pen. Ask Abba to speak to you. Sit quietly for ten minutes (or more) and listen to him in your heart. What is he saying to you about his rest in you? What personal words of love, guidance, or challenge do you hear? Write these out in your journal. (Remember, God's word in your heart will never conflict with his revealed Word in the Bible.)

CLOSING PRAYER: *Dear Abba, thank you that all of my actions can spring forth from the fountain of rest you place at the center of my being. I choose to operate out of your rest and not out of my busyness or ambition. Help me to trust you more. In Jesus' name, Amen.*

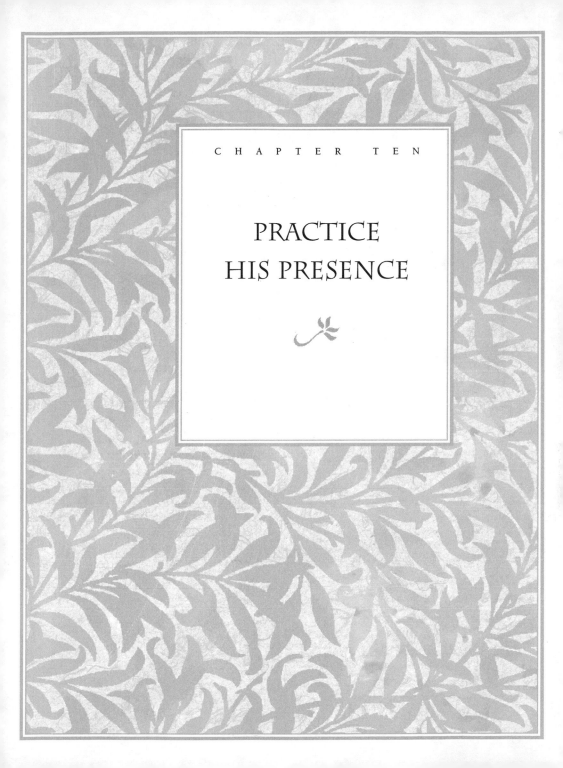

C H A P T E R   T E N

PRACTICE
HIS PRESENCE

PRACTICE HIS PRESENCE

As a writer I'm always fascinated by what makes a book endure. Tens of thousands of books are printed every year, and most of those never see a second printing. In the past eight years I have written eight books, and one of them is already out of print. How I grieved over that little book—it died so young!

Knowing firsthand how much prayer and sweat and lifeblood go into writing a book is what makes me want to know why only a few reach any kind of "maturity" while most meet an early demise, why some hit the mark while most fall far short of the goal. When I pick up a Christian book that has lasted twenty, thirty, or fifty years, I sit up and take notice. I realize there must be something very special on those pages!

One of my very favorite Christian books hit the mark over five hundred years ago, and it's still going strong! It has been affecting people for the kingdom of God for one-fourth of the life of the Christian faith! It was written by a sixteenth-century monk named Brother Lawrence, and it is entitled *The Practice of the Presence of God.*

Brother Lawrence was not an important religious leader or a respected theologian. He was not well educated or well known. He was a very simple man who worked in the kitchen of a monastery scrubbing pots and chopping vegetables.

He never even intended to write a book. His joy was praying as he worked, and his writings were simply letters to friends telling them of his intimate prayer relationship with his Lord and Friend, Jesus Christ. Years later, Brother Lawrence's letters were gathered and published as a book. And that little book with its unlikely, unpretentious origins has lasted for five hundred years.[1]

A SIMPLE SECRET

I believe I know why Brother Lawrence's slim volume of personal testimony has survived for centuries. In it he shared a profound secret—a secret so simple, yet so revolutionary, it has the radical power to change lives.

And what was that secret? Brother Lawrence made it a habit to remind himself all day long of God's presence with him. He taught himself to reflect on the fact that wherever he was, whatever he was doing, God was there—loving him, guiding him, protecting him, encouraging him. He called this secret "practicing God's presence."

This secret is so simple and seemingly obvious that we might tend to discount it. Yet it has proved in my own life to be the pivotal power that can alter the quality of an ordinary day. Whenever I am open to Brother Lawrence's simple secret, it can change any day in my week from one of confusion to one of inner order, from one of chaos to one of peace, from one of depression to one of hope.

When I think of practicing God's presence, I sometimes think of a poem written by my brother, Charlie, which appears in his book *The Well Governed Son*. The poem, entitled "A Walk with My Small Daughter," describes a springtime outing in which he takes his then-three-year-old daughter, Meg, for a walk. With the childlike freedom that comes only from being held in sight of a protective parent, Meg forges out ahead of her dad, bringing back for his inspection the varied treasures of her exploration.

. . . .
She's so sure
I'll always be here she's
willing to leave me a little
at a time, tentative raids
into the world, returning
as we walk, with branch, feather,
flower, bottletop or unnameable
rubber gasket, fragments of
the shared planet, holding them up
for comment, then throwing them
back . . .
She keeps bringing me things
as if I'm an altar. Each we sniff, turn,
taste, name. Each small part a portal
through which to see it all.[2]

I love this word picture, because I believe it depicts the kind of relationship with Abba God that is available to each of us, his children. Each day we share the intimacy of our journey with him. Each day we venture out into the world, but as we go, his loving eyes are always on us. And many times during the day we can run back into his presence, bringing the joys and challenges of our lives as they occur, asking him to help us name and label and understand it all.

A CONSCIOUS AWARENESS

When I speak of "running back into his presence," what do I mean? Aren't we always in his presence? Surely the psalmist stated this in the clearest possible terms.

> Where can I go from your Spirit?
> > Where can I flee from your presence?
> If I go up to the heavens, you are there;
> > if I make my bed in the depths, you are there.
> If I rise on the wings of the dawn,
> > if I settle on the far side of the sea,
> even there your hand will guide me,
> > your right hand will hold me fast. (Ps. 139:7–10 NIV)

No, it is not possible to escape God's presence. But it is possible to close our hearts and minds to it, and when we do, what a radical difference that makes! Like a man dying of thirst who stumbles past a lush oasis, we deprive ourselves of living water when we shut ourselves off from his spirit.

If we yearn for more intimacy with God, if a stronger prayer life is indeed our true desire, we would do well to take Brother Lawrence's humble secret to heart and begin to practice the presence of our Father God.

How, exactly, does one practice his presence in a noisy, busy world? Brother Lawrence lived in a simpler place and time. The kitchen of a country monastery bears no resemblance to the grid-locked freeways and media-congested living rooms we live in. How does the spiritual exercise of this simple, long-ago saint fit into our everyday lives?

In the following pages I share only a few of many ways the ordinary Christian can practice the extraordinary presence of God on a daily basis. I pray that some of these ideas, which have been important in my life, will make a difference in yours.

THE PRESENCE OF HIS REALITY

One of the most obvious ways to practice God's presence is to practice the presence of his reality. There are mornings when I wake up and go to my prayer time, and I don't feel that God is there. Some days I don't even feel that he is real. But I know by faith that he is there and he is real, so I practice the presence of his reality by talking to him at the beginning of my day.

Sometimes I may even use props to help me sense his nearness. I may pull up a chair or set a place at the table for him when I'm eating alone. But with or without props, my decision to talk to him is always an act of faith and obedience. And as I obey, as I open my heart and begin to share my life with him in prayer, I almost always begin to feel him there.

I'll admit that there are times when my feelings refuse to follow my faith like a docile puppy dog, but I don't let that throw me. I just keep on keeping on. I try never to let a lack of feelings rob me of my relationship.

We live in a culture that puts great stock in feelings. Everybody wants to sing about, talk about, and wallow around in feelings. Personally, I think feelings are highly overrated. I mean, I'm glad I have them. And it's great to come across a warm, fuzzy one now and then, but it's nothing to steer your ship by.

The world tries to tell us that if we aren't true to our feelings, we are not being true to ourselves. I have learned from experience that my feelings are the least dependable thing in my world. They are up one day and down the next. How much wiser to be true to God and what he tells me than to bow down to my own erratic feelings.

And what God tells me is this: He tells me he is God and he is here regardless of what I may feel. He is not present because I feel he is present. He is always here, and as I practice the presence of his reality, my heart begins to know what my will has chosen to embrace.

I'll never forget the warm, spring day my friend Jacque, after contemplating a divorce, told me of her conscious decision to stay married to Phillip, her husband of twenty-five years. As many of us do in marriages, both of them had often hurt each other thoughtlessly, becoming insensitive to the other's needs. To Jacque, it felt at the time almost easier to quit than to go back into her damaged relationship, but she chose to stay, believing that God could heal her marriage.

After that decision, there were many months of working through the negative feelings that had grown between them like stubborn weeds in a garden. But as they practiced the presence of God's reality in their home, both Jacque and Phillip began to experience God's restoration in their marriage.

The Bible tells us we can put on faith or praise or love like a garment. It is a deliberate act that many times has nothing to do with feelings. J. B. Phillips's translation of Ephesians 4:22–24 exhorts us "to fling off the dirty clothes of the old way of living, which were rotted through and through with lust's illusions, and, with yourselves mentally and spiritually re-made, to put on the clean, fresh clothes of the new life which was made by God's design for righteousness and the holiness which is no illusion."

When practicing God's presence in your prayer time with him, you may even choose to symbolize this deliberate act of "putting on" by actually putting on a favorite comfortable bathrobe or a soft sweater. As you do, tell Abba God that you are choosing now to put on your faith in his reality as you come into his presence.

THE PRESENCE OF HIS POWER

Another aspect of his presence we would do well to practice is the presence of his power. There is so much more power available to us in Jesus Christ than we generally acknowledge or act on.

The topic of available power puts me in mind of a guy I was in college with, who loved working on "hot cars." I didn't know this guy personally, but he was something of a legend on our campus. One of his more famous capers involved removing the tiny, putt-putt engine from the back of a Volkswagen Beetle (along with the car's backseat) and replacing it with the powerful engine of a Porsche. Rumor had it that he loved to chug up to a stoplight and challenge some power-mobile in the next lane to "drag." The unsuspecting owner of the larger car was always left in the dust by the little Beetle with the macho engine!

Our lives, once surrendered to the Lord, are a lot like that little "power Beetle." We don't just get a tune-up or even a few new parts. The Bible tells us that, once we've put God in the driver's seat, he pulls out the old life and replaces it with a whole new infinitely more powerful one—his own! ("Therefore, if anyone is in Christ, he is a new creation; the old has gone, the new has come!"—2 Cor. 5:17 NIV.)

This new "replacement" life gives us power, not only over death someday, but power in the midst of life *right now*. It is a present-tense power-packed Porsche engine capable of overcoming the big and little challenges of today! The problem is, many of us continue to drive like Volkswagens, chugging along about twenty-five miles an hour through life because we forget to practice the presence of the Power that is "under our hoods." We never cash in on the promise of 1 Thessalonians 5:24, which tells us, "the one who calls you is faithful and he will do it" (NIV).

One of the most life-changing experiences on my Christian journey has been my participation for the past two years on the prayer team of my local church. We have studied some great books on prayer and have attended some exciting conferences. But by far the most life-changing part of these two years has been spent actually praying for ourselves and others and seeing God's power to change hearts and lives.

This exact same power is present when we meet Abba God in our personal prayer time. We need to come expectantly, reminding ourselves of how much power he has made available to us in his Son, Jesus Christ, and through his indwelling Holy Spirit. Would we sit calmly in a room with an earthquake or a tornado and expect nothing to happen? We serve the God who created earthquakes and tornadoes! And he has put that same intensity of spiritual energy and authority at our disposal when we choose to practice the presence of his power in us. We are reminded in 2 Corinthians 4:7 that "we have this treasure [his Spirit] in jars of clay [our bodies] to show that this all-surpassing power is from God and not from us" (NIV).

PRACTICE THE PRESENCE OF HIS GUIDANCE

If you have ever memorized a psalm, it was probably the beautiful twenty-third, which assures us that the Lord is our Shepherd who leads and guides us. The Bible is full of assurances of God's guidance. Psalm 48:14 says, "This God is our God forever and ever. He will guide us from now on." Proverbs 4:11 assures us, "I am guiding you in the way of wisdom, and I am leading you on the right path." The words of Isaiah promise in verse 58:11, "The LORD will guide you always; he will satisfy your needs in a sun-scorched land and will strengthen your frame. You will be like a well-watered garden, like a spring whose waters never fail" (NIV). And most precious of all to me is the promise Jesus makes to us in John 16:13: "But when the Spirit of truth comes, he will lead you into all truth. He will not speak his own words, but he will speak only what he hears, and he will tell you what is to come." As we practice the presence of God's guidance in the midst of the daily confusion of life, he will prove these things to be true again and again.

My longtime friend Chris Kelly has practiced the presence of God's guidance in a million daily ways since her husband, Pat, was diagnosed with non-Hodgkins lymphoma and died earlier this year. When Pat had to undergo chemotherapy at Vanderbilt University Medical Center in Nashville, Chris had to leave six of her children at home in Mobile while she spent time in Nashville with Pat. One of the most challenging parts of Chris's ordeal was her daily task of navigating through rush-hour traffic from the suburb of Brentwood into the city where the hospital was located. As she was driving one morning, she began to feel certain she had made a wrong turn.

"Show me, Lord, how to proceed," she prayed. "Am I on the right road, or should I turn around?" At that precise moment on the Christian radio station she was listening to, her favorite singer, Billy Sprague, began to sing a song she loves called "Press On." That was her answer. She stayed steady on her course, confident that the road would lead her to the hospital. And it did. Those who have never practiced the presence of God's guidance might call this a coincidence. We who know him know it is not. He is the Shepherd who leads in every small detail of life.

PRACTICE THE PRESENCE OF HIS REDEMPTION

On a silent retreat during a bleak, freezing week in March years ago, I learned a beautiful, new way to practice the presence of God's redemption. The retreat was led by a Franciscan brother we were invited to call "Brother Bob," or simply "Bob."

Bob had grown up in Chicago in a neighborhood near the stockyards, where he and his friends would often play. There they grew accustomed to the sight of animals being slaughtered.

But there was one particular yard in which the process of preparing the animals was quite different. In this yard, the animals were not only slaughtered but "bled" until no blood remained in the meat. Bob found that this was where the kosher meats were prepared for the Jewish community.

Long years after those childhood trips to the stockyards, Bob had an opportunity to ask a rabbi about the significance of bleeding the animals. The rabbi explained to Bob that the Jews of Bible times believed that the life was in the blood. They believed that to eat meat that contained the blood of an animal was to take in its properties and could cause you to behave and become like that animal.

It was then that Brother Bob's eyes were opened in a new way to the meaningful symbol that Jesus extended to us at the Eucharistic feast. By inviting us to partake of his body and his blood, he was holding out to us the very essence of his life and character. He was inviting us to partake of his perfection, to become like him, to take in the very qualities of his life. He was inviting us to come to his table and make a trade with him—to give him our brokenness and take in his wholeness, to give him our fear and take in his faith, to give him our hatred and take in his love.

In our personal prayer time, we can practice the presence of his redemption by individually reflecting on the Lord's powerful gift with gratitude and amazement. He made himself present to us in the symbol of his own blood. He gave himself so that we could be like him. He went to Calvary so that we could come freely to the Father, moving from the outer fringe of the crowd into the welcoming arms of his acceptance.

Whether we walk confidently into the "Holy of Holies," sure of God's love, or whether we crawl wearily onto his lap with scraped knees and tattered egos, we can always come to him, and say, "Hi, God. It's me." We can receive the only love and forgiveness that renews our faith and restores our souls.

He is always there for us—all of us: brilliant and feeble-minded, leaders and followers, rich and poor, all colors, all ages, ALL! He's done his part, and now he waits. The only thing we have to do is accept his life-changing invitation.

One year my friend Anne Hunt had a beautiful quotation calligraphied at Christmas for her friends. Written by renowned nineteenth-century preacher Phillips Brooks, it is rich in meaning for me, and over the years I have meditated on it many times. I share it here, in part, because it speaks so strongly about this ever-available gift of intimacy with God the Father:

> The great danger facing all of us . . . is not that
> we shall make an absolute failure of life, nor

that we shall fall into outright viciousness,
nor that we shall be terribly unhappy, nor that
we shall feel that life has no meaning at all . . .
The danger is that we may fail to perceive life's
greatest meaning, fall short of its highest good,
miss its deepest and most abiding happiness,
be unable to render the most needed service,
be unconscious of life ablaze with the light
of the Presence of God—and be content to
have it so—that is the danger. That someday
we may wake up and find that always we have
been busy with the husks and trappings of
life—and have really missed life itself. For
life without God, to one who has known the
richness and joy of life with Him, is unthinkable,
impossible. That is what one prays one's
friends may be spared—satisfaction with a life
that falls short of the best, that has in it no
tingle and thrill which comes from a friendship with the Father.

If a friendship with the Father is what we want, we must come to
him as little children—past all the grown-up theological concepts
and religious ideas that crowd outside a real knowledge of him,
through the veil that has been ripped asunder by our Savior's loving
hands, and into the awesome and intimate presence of our Abba,
who waits where we may say to him with all confidence:

"Hi, God. It's us. Your kids."

PRACTICE HIS PRESENCE: 1
PRAYER IS SHARING YOUR LIFE

*Read and reflect on these verses of Scripture
and the letter from your Abba that follows.*

LORD, every morning you hear my voice.
Every morning, I tell you what I need,
and I wait for your answer. PS. 5:3

And in praying, do not heap up empty phrases as the Gentiles do; for
they think that they will be heard for their many words. MATT. 6:7 RSV

Dear Child,

*Prayer is a daily way of sharing your life with me. It's that simple. You
don't have to be an expert on prayer to pray. I am not grading you like a
teacher with a red pencil. I am not moved by intellectual words or poetic
language. I just want to be with you. Release yourself from the need to
achieve a great, impressive prayer life, and just give yourself permission
to practice my presence. Be aware of how near I am to you. Talk to me as
someone you trust. Take me into every situation. All that I ask for is your
honesty. All that I long for is your company. Come to me. Bring your secret
failures and your sad regrets. Bring your hopes and your happiness. Bring
yourself to share with me. And you will find me waiting—a Father you
can trust and a Friend you can depend on.*

Ever your,
Abba

WRITE A LETTER TO YOUR ABBA: 1

PRAYERS OF ENTERING IN

*After reading and reflecting on God's words to you,
write your own letter to him, using the following guide:*

1. In your journal or in the space below, share with Abba God your desire
   to be more aware of him in everyday ways. Think of some ways you
   can practice his presence tomorrow. Ask him to ride with you in the
   car, to be with you as you work or cook, etc.

Dear Abba,

_____

_____

_____

_____

_____

2. Put down your pen. Ask Abba God to speak to you. Then sit quietly
   for ten minutes (or more) and listen for him in your heart. What is he
   saying to you today about practicing his presence? What personal
   words of love, guidance, or challenge do you hear? Write out in your
   journal any words, phrases, or sentences he speaks to you. (Remember,
   God's word in your heart will never contradict his revealed Word in the
   Bible.)

   CLOSING PRAYER: *Dear Abba, open my eyes to you in everything I
   do. Let me remember your reality all around me and your Spirit within
   me. I don't want to miss the excitement of living this life to the fullest
   with and for you. Amen.*

PRACTICE HIS PRESENCE: 2

BE AT HOME IN ME

Do not be anxious about anything, but in everything, by prayer and petition, with thanksgiving, present your requests to God. And the peace of God, which transcends all understanding, will guard your hearts and your minds in Christ Jesus. PHIL. 4:6–7 NIV

For in him we live and move and have our being. ACTS 17:28 NIV

Dearest Child,

Let prayer become the breath of your spirit. Let it be the beating of your heart. Be aware of my presence at all times. Come simply before Me without anxiety and let the roots of your spirit go deep. Remain in a thankful awareness of my nearness all day as you work at the gentle occupation of being my child. And a deep, sweet peace will stand guard over your thoughts and your emotions as you live and move and have your being in me. That is when your heart will discover that to live a whole day in the awareness of my presence is the loveliest prayer of all!

Be at home in me,
Abba

WRITE A LETTER TO YOUR ABBA: 2

PRAYERS OF ENTERING IN

1. In your letter to Abba God, ask him to help you spend this whole day in a thankful awareness of his presence. Thank him for his blessings that surround you—not only the big things but also the small ones. The sound of birdsong, the smell of coffee, the laughter of a child. When you have thanked him for the good things, thank him for the hard things and the challenges, too. Thank him for being with you in every part of your life today and every day.

Dear Abba,

_____

_____

_____

_____

_____

2. Now put down your pen. Ask Abba God to speak to you. Then sit quietly for ten minutes (or more) and listen for his voice. What is he saying to you today about being thankfully aware of his nearness? What personal words of love, guidance, or challenge do you hear? Write out in your journal any words, phrases, or sentences you hear in your heart. (Remember, God's word in your heart will never contradict his revealed Word in the Bible.)

CLOSING PRAYER: *Dear Abba, help me not to take for granted the fact that you allow me to spend my day in your presence. Keep the eyes of my spirit open to you all day as I go about the gentle occupation of being your child today. I love you, Lord. Amen.*

PRACTICE HIS PRESENCE: 3

PRAYER IS A NECESSITY

Call to me and I will answer you and tell you great and unsearchable things you do not know. JER. 33:3 NIV

God is spirit, and his worshipers must worship in spirit and in truth. JOHN 4:24 NIV

My Child,

I encourage you to pray. You are a spiritual being, and to a spiritual being, prayer is not a luxury, it is a necessity. To live without prayer is to exist in a tangle of illusions. But when you stay in my presence, I continually quiet you with my truth. In my presence you can see things clearly. Your choices become more simple and your way more straight. When you seek me in prayer, you will find me always available, always waiting to give you my attention, never too tired or rushed to spend time with you. My favorite time of day is the time I hear you calling my name! So, come. Practice my presence.

Your Father and Friend,
Abba

WRITE A LETTER TO YOUR ABBA: 3

PRAYERS OF ENTERING IN

1. In your letter, tell Abba God about your prayer life. Do you have trouble praying? Try to determine why. Time? Attention? Ask him to show you Brother Lawrence's secret so that you can begin to see prayer as an ongoing daily awareness.

Dear Abba,

_____

_____

_____

_____

_____

_____

_____

2. Now put down your pen. Ask Abba to speak to you. Sit quietly for ten minutes (or more) and listen to him in your heart. What is he saying to you about the importance of personal prayer? What personal words of love, guidance, or challenge do you hear? Write these out in your journal. (Remember, God's word in your heart will never conflict with his revealed Word in the Bible.)

CLOSING PRAYER: *Dear Abba, thank you for the gift of prayer. Thank you that you are always available to me—that you never make me wait or put me on hold. Help me to be more available to you. As I keep the eyes of my heart open to you, help me to enjoy your presence more and more. I love you, Lord. Amen.*

PRACTICE HIS PRESENCE: 4

BRING ALL TO ME

Taste and see that the LORD is good;
    blessed is the man who takes refuge in him. Ps. 34:8 NIV

Those who look to him are radiant;
    their faces are never covered with shame. Ps. 34:5 NIV

My Child,

    Come into my presence today. Take refuge in me and experience my goodness. Look to me in every situation, and your face will be radiant. When your heart is empty and aching, you will find fullness and healing in me. When your spirit is brimming with joy, I will be there to share it with you. Whether the future looks bright and hopeful or the way ahead looks impassable, whether your dreams are as clear as glass or as murky as a mud puddle, see me here. Know my nearness. Bring all to me—every trial and every triumph, every hope and every fear, every burden and every blessing. Live every moment in my presence.

Your loving Abba,
God

WRITE A LETTER TO YOUR ABBA: 4

PRAYERS OF ENTERING IN

1. As you write your letter to Abba God, consciously bring into his presence all of yourself. Write out all the jobs you must do and all the "roles" you must play (roles such as "parent," "friend," "stockbroker," "Sunday school teacher," etc.). In writing, acknowledge your need for him in each of these roles. Beside each role you may wish to list the ways you need God. For instance, beside "parent" you may wish to write "more patience, less complaining," etc.

Dear Abba,

2. Now put down your pen. Ask Abba God to speak to you. Then sit quietly for ten minutes (or more) and listen for him in your heart. What is he saying to you today about bringing his presence into each part of your life? What personal words of love, guidance, or challenge do you hear? Write these out in your journal. (Remember, God's word in your heart will never contradict his revealed Word in the Bible.)

CLOSING PRAYER: *Dear Abba, I bring into your presence all that I am. I give you all of my successes and all of my failures. Be present in all of my strengths and my weaknesses today. Fill me and anoint me to operate as your person in each area of my life. And as I trust you, make me more like your Son. I pray in his name, Amen.*

PRACTICE HIS PRESENCE: 5

WALK BY FAITH

Then Jesus told him, "Because you have seen me, you have believed; blessed are those who have not seen and yet have believed." JOHN 20:29 NIV

Let us draw near to God with a sincere heart in full assurance of faith." HEB. 10:22A NIV

This is the victory that has overcome the world, even our faith. 1 JOHN 5:4B NIV

My Child,

Every day I reveal to you more of who I am, and every day I encourage you to believe. As you spend more and more of your time in my presence, your faith is strengthened. Faith is not a feeling but a choice—a decision of the will that propels the personality, the entire character of a person, to move toward me and my kingdom. I am not saying that you won't experience wonderful feelings of assurance and joy. These will come to you on some days, yes. But there will be days when your feelings will tug in total opposition to belief. Then belief in me must be a choice. When the voices of the world tell you things that contradict my Word, always choose to believe my Word, for it will tell you the truth about who I am. Believe in me and . . .

Walk by faith,
Abba

WRITE A LETTER TO YOUR ABBA: 5

PRAYERS OF ENTERING IN

1. In your letter to Abba God, reflect on whether your life has been based on feelings or faith. Remember times when your feelings have caused you to choose certain things or act in certain ways. How did those choices or actions affect you? How can practicing God's presence make a difference in current and future choices?

Dear Abba,

_____

_____

_____

_____

_____

_____

_____

_____

2. Now put down your pen. Ask Abba God to speak to you. Sit quietly for ten minutes (or more) and listen for him in your heart. What is he saying to you about choosing to walk by faith? What personal words of love, guidance, or challenge do you hear? Write these out in your journal. (Remember, God's word in your heart will never conflict with his revealed Word in the Bible.)

CLOSING PRAYER: *Abba God, thank you for designing a relationship with me based on my faith in who you are. Thank you for the gift of faith. I ask you to strengthen me to choose to walk by faith every day as I live my life in your presence. Amen.*

NOTES

A Hunger for Intimacy

1. C. S. Lewis, *Letters to Malcolm: Chiefly on Prayer* (New York: Harcourt, Brace, and World, 1964), 22.

Chapter 1. Know Him As Your Abba

1. Richard Foster, *Celebration of Discipline* (San Francisco: Harper, 1978, 1988), 159–60.
2. A. W. Tozer, *The Best of Tozer* (Grand Rapids, MI: Baker, 1978), 120.
3. Les Christie, "Finish the Race," in *Hot Illustrations for Youth Talks* (El Cajon, CA: Youth Specialties Books, 1994), 93.

Chapter 2. Let Him Have Your Life

1. Author unknown, "The Road of Life," quoted in Tim Hansel, *Holy Sweat* (Waco, TX: Word, 1987).
2. Richard Foster, *Prayer: Finding the Heart's True Home* (San Francisco: Harper, 1992), 47–48.
3. Larry J. Hein, S.J., quoted in "New Year's Note from Brennan 'n' Roslyn," *Brennan Manning Newsletter,* January 1991.
4. Abraham Joshua Heschel, *Man's Quest for God* (New York: Scribner-Macmillan, 1981), quoted in Benson and Benson, *Disciplines for the Inner Life,* 66.

5. Lawrence Cunningham, *Francis of Assisi* (San Francisco: Scala/Harper and Row, 1981), 12–13.

6. A. W. Tozer, *The Pursuit of God* (Harrisburg, PA: Christian Publications, 1948), 23, 31.

7. Tilden H. Edwards, *Living Simply Through the Day* (Ramsey, NJ: Paulist Press, 1977).

Chapter 3. Worship with Your Whole Heart

1. Foster, *Celebration of Discipline,* 158.

2. "Even the Praise Comes from You," by Claire Cloninger and Lynn Keesecker, © Copyright 1983 by Manna Music, Inc. Used by permission.

3. Oswald Chambers, *My Utmost for His Highest* (Grand Rapids, MI: Discovery House, 1992), Jan. 6.

4. Signa Bodishbaugh, *Journey to Wholeness in Christ* (Wheaton, IL: Chosen Books, 1997), 71–75.

5. Merlin R. Carothers, *Power in Praise* (Escondido, CA: Merlin R. Carothers Publishing, 1972), 6.

6. Foster, *Celebration of Discipline,* 168.

7. Andy's group, Dog Named David, has released its first CD, "It's Alright," which can be ordered by writing to Dog Named David Music, P. O. Box 16423, Mobile, AL 36616, or calling 334–476–0301.

8. Foster, *Celebration of Discipline,* 167.

9. Chambers, *My Utmost For His Highest,* Sept. 10.

Chapter 4. Walk in His Forgiveness

1. My ideas on "missing the target" were shaped by reading William Barclay, *The Gospel of Matthew,* vol. 1, rev. ed. (Philadelphia: Westminster, 1975), 220.

2. David Watson, *Called and Committed* (Wheaton, IL: Harold Shaw Publishers, 1982), 91.

3. Leanne Payne, *Restoring the Christian Soul Through Healing Prayer* (Wheaton, IL: Good News, 1991), 26–27.

4. Watson, *Called and Committed,* 92.
5. Giacomo Puccini, quoted in Julia Cameron, *The Artist's Way: A Spiritual Path to Higher Creativity* (New York: G. P. Putnam's Sons, 1992), 2.

Chapter 5. Listen for His Voice

1. Leanne Payne, *Listening Prayer: Learning to Hear God's Voice and Keep a Prayer Journal* (Grand Rapids, MI: Hamewith Books, 1994), 132.
2. Linda Schubert, *Miracle Hour: A Method of Prayer That Will Change Your Life* (Santa Clara, CA: Miracles of the Heart Ministries, 1992), 25.
3. Author unknown, *The Cloud of Unknowing and Other Works,* translated with an introduction by Clifton Wolters (London: Penguin Books, 1961, 1978), 83.
4. Watson, *Called and Committed,* 106.
5. To find out more about Crown Ministries Small Group Financial Studies, contact Crown Ministries, 530 Crown Oak Center Dr., Longwood, FL 32750. Telephone: 407-331-6000.
6. J. I. Packer, quoted in Watson, *Called and Committed.*
7. Brennan Manning, *Abba's Child: The Cry of the Heart for Intimate Belonging* (Colorado Springs: Navpress, 1994), 127-28.
8. Payne, *Listening Prayer,* 169.

Chapter 6. Accept His Acceptance

1. Henri J. M. Nouwen, *Life of the Beloved* (New York: Crossroad, 1992), 21.
2. Payne, *Restoring the Christian Soul through Healing Prayer,* 32.
3. Anabel Gillham, *The Confident Woman: Knowing Who You Are in Christ* (Eugene, OR: Harvest House, 1993), 28-29.

Chapter 7. Let Him Love through You

1. Dr. V. Raymond Edman, "Meet the Major," an introduction to Major W. Ian Thomas, *The Saving Life of Christ* (Grand Rapids, MI: Zondervan, 1961), 7-9.

2. Walter C. Lanyon, *The Laughter of God* (Union Life Ministries, 1977), 9–10.

Chapter 8. Trust Him in the Fight

1. Bishop John Howe, a taped series on spiritual warfare recorded at Truro Episcopal Church, Fairfax, Virginia. I am indebted to Bishop Howe's teaching tape on the armor of God from which a number of ideas in this chapter are taken.
2. David and Karen Mains, *Tales of the Kingdom* (Elgin, IL: Chariot Books, 1983), 74–80.
3. "A River Met a Mountain," words and music by Andy Cloninger, (c) Dog Named David Music, 1994.
4. Manning, *Abba's Child,* 169.

Chapter 9. Enter His Rest

1. Foster, *Prayer: Finding the Heart's True Home,* 93.
2. Frederick Buechner, *The Hungering Dark* (San Francisco: Harper, 1969), 74–75.
3. Micki Ann Harris, "December 22," *Prepare Ye the Way of the Lord* (Mobile, AL: Christ Episcopal Church Advent Devotional, 1996).
4. Robert A. Cloninger, "Morning Song," © 1985.
5. Meister Eckhart, quoted in Thomas R. Kelly, *A Testament of Devotion* (San Francisco: Harper, 1992), 3.

Chapter 10. Practice His Presence

1. Brother Lawrence of the Resurrection, *The Practice of the Presence of God* (New York: Walker, 1974).
2. Charles deGravelles, *The Well Governed Son* (New Orleans: New Orleans Poetry Journal Press, 1987).